Acts

CHARLES C. WILLIAMSON

Geneva Press
Louisville, Kentucky

Book design by Drew Stevens
Cover design by Pam Poll
Cover illustration by Robert Stratton

First edition
Published by Geneva Press
Louisville, Kentucky

This book is printed on acid-free paper that meets the American National Standards Institute Z39.48 standard. ♾

PRINTED IN THE UNITED STATES OF AMERICA

00 01 02 03 04 05 06 07 08 09 — 10 9 8 7 6 5 4 3 2 1

Library of Congress Cataloging-in-Publication Data

A catalog record for this book is available from the Library of Congress.

ISBN 0-664-50105-2

Contents

Series Introduction

The Bible has long been revered for its witness to God's presence and redeeming activity in the world; its message of creation and judgment, love and forgiveness, grace and hope; its memorable characters and stories; its challenges to human life; and its power to shape faith. For generations people have found in the Bible inspiration and instruction, and, for nearly as long, commentators and scholars have assisted students of the Bible. This series, Interpretation Bible Studies (IBS), continues that great heritage of scholarship with a fresh approach to biblical study.

Designed for ease and flexibility of use for either personal or group study, IBS helps readers not only to learn about the history and theology of the Bible, understand the sometimes difficult language of biblical passages, and marvel at the biblical accounts of God's activity in human life, but also to accept the challenge of the Bible's call to discipleship. IBS offers sound guidance for deepening one's knowledge of the Bible and for faithful Christian living in today's world.

IBS was developed out of three primary convictions. First, the Bible is the church's scripture and stands in a unique place of authority in Christian understanding. Second, good scholarship helps readers understand the truths of the Bible and sharpens their perception of God speaking through the Bible. Third, deep knowledge of the Bible bears fruit in one's ethical and spiritual life.

Each IBS volume has ten brief units of key passages from a book of the Bible. By moving through these units, readers capture the sweep of the whole biblical book. Each unit includes study helps, such as maps, photos, definitions of key terms, questions for reflection, and suggestions for resources for further study. In the back of each volume is a Leader's Guide that offers helpful suggestions on how to use IBS.

The Interpretation Bible Studies series grows out of the well-known Interpretation commentaries (John Knox Press), a series that helps preachers and teachers in their preparation. Although each IBS volume bears a deep kinship to its companion Interpretation commentary, IBS can stand alone. The reader need not be familiar with the Interpretation commentary to benefit from IBS. However, those who want to discover even more about the Bible will benefit by consulting Interpretation commentaries too.

Through the kind of encounter with the Bible encouraged by the Interpretation Bible Studies, the church will continue to discover God speaking afresh in the scriptures.

Introduction to Acts

From the very opening sentence, readers of Acts realize that they are being dropped into the middle of a larger story. It's a story that begins in the Gospel of Luke, telling about the earthly ministry of Jesus, and now continues as a two-volume work in Acts. In Luke we hear the teachings of Jesus, see his miraculous deeds, and witness his life of faith and servanthood. We celebrate Jesus' birth, grieve at his death, and rejoice in his victory over death. In Luke we are introduced to the band of disciples who were called by Jesus to leave behind their fishing nets and the other activities that occupied their lives to follow Jesus. We watch with interest as these disciples come to the amazing conclusion that Jesus is unique, unlike anyone they have ever met before.

The writer of the Gospel of Luke knew, however, that the story of Jesus did not end with the resurrection of Jesus. The resurrection was a new beginning. That is where Acts takes up. In Acts the focus shifts away from Jesus and his earthly ministry, to the work of the disciples under the guidance and leading of the Holy Spirit. Although the book is called "The Acts of the Apostles," many have suggested that a better title would be "The Acts of the Holy Spirit." The story told in Acts recounts time and time again the miraculous working of the Holy Spirit in the lives of real people.

> "The story told here is open-ended, because it continues today in your church and mine."—William H. Willimon, *Acts*, Interpretation (Atlanta: John Knox Press, 1988), 1.

There are a number of clues that lead a reader to conclude that the Gospel of Luke and the book of Acts were written by the same hand. Perhaps the most obvious is that both are addressed to Theophilus (Luke 1:3;

Acts 1:1). But there are other clues as well. Bible scholars have noted a similar writing style in both books. Some have also observed a similar structure in both Luke and Acts. Luke, for example, begins with the birth of Jesus, Acts with the birth of the church. Luke describes the mission and ministry of Jesus; Acts describes the mission and ministry of the early church. Jesus' trial in Luke parallels Paul's trial in Acts (Walaskay, 7–8). For this reason, commentaries often refer to "Luke-Acts" to underscore the connection between the two books.

When we read Acts, what are we reading? What type of literature is Acts? It's not a Gospel, like Luke's first volume. A Gospel tells the good news of God's saving work in the life, death, and resurrection of Jesus. Acts is not that, although it certainly contains good news. Nor is Acts a letter, like the letters of Paul found elsewhere in the New Testament. To call Acts a history book is not quite accurate either. It is a unique category of literature that tells the story of the New Testament church in its particular historical and geographical setting and that, at the same time, tells of the life-changing work of the Holy Spirit. Acts does not pretend to give an unbiased historical account of the occurrences in first-century Palestine. Rather, its purpose, like that of Luke, is to persuade, to challenge, and to proclaim good news by recounting the work of the Holy Spirit in the life of the New Testament church.

> "When asked by unbelievers, 'How do we know your gospel is true?' we must, like Acts, trot out not only our little arguments for inspection but also our little lives. The best support any of us can give these stories is the way we back them up with the lives we lead."—William H. Willimon, *Acts*, Interpretation, 4.

The issues the New Testament church faced created many hurdles for the growing church to cross. Who could be admitted into the fellowship? Were the Gentiles welcome or was the church only for those who had been raised in the traditions of the Old Testament heroes, such as Abraham and Sarah, Moses and Miriam? What was the Christian church's relationship to its Jewish heritage? What would life look like among the followers of Jesus? How could the story of the saving work of Jesus best be communicated to the people of the larger Roman world with its pantheon of gods and its many and varied philosophies? The questions were numerous and the challenges great, yet the believers discovered that they were not alone as they faced these formidable issues. They were enabled by a power beyond themselves, and sometimes that power took them to some surprising places. The story of Acts tells of the always powerful, and often unpredictable, leading of the Holy Spirit.

As we read about the work of the Holy Spirit in the stories of Acts, we cannot help but feel ourselves being drawn into the story, as if it is also our story. And this is no accident. Both Luke and Acts are addressed to someone named Theophilus. No one really knows who Theophilus was. Perhaps he was Luke's benefactor or patron. It is also possible that Theophilus was not one individual, but the church. The name Theophilus means "Lover of God," and thus Acts could have been written with all "lovers of God" in mind. If that is so, then Acts was written for us modern-day readers as well as the first-century readers. No wonder we are drawn into the story; it was written to us.

Luke also states that this is the story of those "witnesses in Jerusalem, in all Judea and Samaria, and to the ends of the earth" (1:8). Luke could have intended this to be understood to apply to a specific geographic region of the world and that Acts tells how the story of Jesus was spread through the entire known world at that time. However, Luke could have had something bigger in mind. The phrase "to the ends of the earth" can also be understood symbolically, and perhaps it is Luke's way of saying that the story of the followers of Jesus has no end, and that it will be told in places and times that Luke could not even imagine. And indeed that has been true. The story told in Acts is now our story.

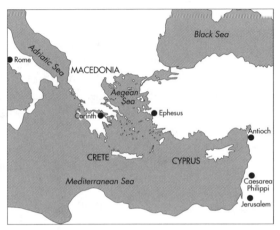

Acts is the account of the expansion of the church into the world.

Reading Acts draws us into the story in yet another way. As we read about the work of the Holy Spirit in the lives of Peter and Paul, Philip and Stephen, Priscilla and Aquila, and many others—some well known, and others less so—we find ourselves wondering how we might act and what we might say in such circumstances. When we read how Peter was forced to broaden his thinking about the early church's relationship to the Gentiles, we present-day readers are forced to ask about our church's relationship to those who are considered unwelcome. As the early church struggled with the meaning of life together in community, the modern reader inevitably asks the same questions today.

Finally, we modern-day readers are engaged and drawn into the story told in Acts when we realize that the story of the church and the followers of Jesus is open-ended. It doesn't end with Paul in Rome. One could say that there have been many subsequent volumes as through the centuries the stories of the work of the Holy Spirit in the lives of real people continue to be written. The story told in Acts is in a very real way the story of every believer. Acts tells about people—people talking to other people, telling about how they have experienced God's work in their lives. Still today that is the way the good news of Jesus is spread. In huge cathedrals with pipe organs and stained glass windows, the story of Jesus is told. In house churches as friends gather, the story is told. In living rooms over a cup of coffee as a believer shares with a friend experiences of God's love, the story is told. The book of Acts is simply the beginning of this person-to-person telling and retelling of the story of Jesus.

Acts is full of wonderful stories of the early church, more than can fit within the confines of this study. The story of Stephen, the first Christian martyr (Acts 6–7); the story of Simon the magician (Acts 8); the story of Philip and the Ethiopian official (also Acts 8); and the story of Paul and Silas singing hymns in the Philippian jail (Acts 16) are left for the student to study on his or her own. Students of Acts will want to find their way to these stories to broaden their understanding of this important book.

One who wants to dig deeper into the study of Acts will find it helpful to consult a commentary that gives a fuller introduction about the authorship, setting, and purpose of Acts. Two commentaries worth noting are William Willimon's commentary in the Interpretation series and Paul Walaskay's commentary in the Westminster Bible Companion series. Both are very readable.

This particular book has come about by a group effort. I meet weekly with a group of clergy (Steve Caddell, pastor of South Mecklenburg Presbyterian Church in Charlotte, North Carolina; Art Gatewood, pastor of Grace Presbyterian Church in Fort Mill, South Carolina; Todd Hobbie, pastor of First Presbyterian

Want to Know More?

About leading Bible study groups? See Roberta Hestenes, *Using the Bible in Groups* (Philadelphia: Westminster Press, 1983).

About studying the book of Acts? See William H. Willimon, *Acts,* Interpretation; Paul W. Walaskay, *Acts,* Westminster Bible Companion (Louisville, Ky.: Westminster John Knox Press, 1998); and William Barclay, *The Acts of the Apostles,* Daily Study Bible (Philadelphia: Westminster Press, 1976).

About the common authorship of Luke and Acts? See G. H. C. Macgregor, *Acts,* Interpreter's Bible, vol. 9 (Nashville: Abingdon Press, 1954), 3–5; for a more technical discussion, see Ernst Haenchen, *The Acts of the Apostles: A Commentary* (Philadelphia: Westminster Press, 1971), 3–14.

Church, Concord, North Carolina; and Tom Tate, pastor of Plaza Presbyterian Church in Charlotte, North Carolina) who have the regular—and sometimes relentless—task of preaching and teaching. For ten weeks following Easter in 1999 we agreed to focus on these particular texts in Acts. Several questions helped us to get into the study of a particular passage:

- If this passage were omitted from the Bible, what would we be missing?
- What did this passage do for those first-century Christians?
- What does it do for us as twenty-first-century Christians?
- How does this passage address the needs and concerns of the members of our churches today?

This process and the free discussion by the group helped make the passages come alive. We invite you to join us in the discussion. As we continue to learn about the life of the early Christian church and those early followers of Jesus, may we find our own lives of faith and service enriched.

1 Acts 1:1–26

New Beginnings

The forty days that followed Easter must have been wonderful for the disciples—especially wonderful considering what had gone before. Those terrible last days before the crucifixion of Jesus had been terrible for the disciples as well. Some of the disciples could not bear to watch, or perhaps they lacked the courage to stay around, as Jesus underwent the sham of a trial, endured the mockery and ridicule of the soldiers, and died the agonizing death by crucifixion. When Jesus breathed his last, the cause to which the disciples had given their lives during the preceding three years died too. Or so it seemed.

> "Death, the ultimate 'ending'—the master fact which determines most of our horizons, our values, our projects—has been ended in the resurrection of Christ."—William H. Willimon, *Acts,* Interpretation, 19–20.

But then came that Sunday morning when the word began to spread among the women and the disciples that the body of Jesus was missing from the tomb. Some people were even saying that Jesus was alive. Indeed, Jesus was alive! He appeared to the disciples.

Forty Days

In the Gospel of Luke the writer of Luke-Acts tells of two resurrection appearances. One is the familiar story of the travelers walking from Jerusalem to Emmaus, found in Luke 24:13–35. The other is that Easter evening appearance when suddenly Jesus was there with the disciples (24:36–49). This opening chapter of Acts records that in the days between Easter and Jesus' ascension into heaven, Jesus appeared to the disciples a number of times.

Unfortunately, the Gospel writers give only scant information about these resurrection appearances. One may occasionally hear someone say something like, "If Jesus would appear to me, then I would believe. But until I have proof, I will not believe." Like Thomas in the Gospel of John (20:24–29), some people find it difficult to believe in the resurrection of Jesus without concrete "proof." Believers today would like to know more about these "many convincing proofs" (Acts 1:3).

The time period "forty days" will have a familiar ring to students of the Bible. Moses spent forty days on Mount Sinai receiving God's law (Ex. 34:28). Elijah was on Mount Horeb for forty days when he heard "the still small voice of God" (1 Kings 19:8). Jesus was led by the Spirit into the wilderness, where he stayed for forty days and where he was "tempted by the devil" (Luke 4:2). Paul Walaskay calls this "sacred time" (Walaskay, 26). Just as Moses, Elijah, and even Jesus himself spent time in the presence of God receiving God's guidance, here at the beginning of Acts we are told that the disciples spent that sacred time in the presence of the resurrected Christ receiving guidance for what was yet to come.

Here then is one of the interesting parallels between Luke and Acts. Early in Luke we are told that Jesus spent forty days in the wilderness away from the crowds and the activities that would fill his life in the days to come. Now here in the opening chapter of Acts, we see the disciples doing the same thing. In both cases it was a necessary step in their preparation for the work of ministry that lay ahead. Many Christians today have discovered the spiritual value of just such a retreat away from the busyness and pressures of the world in order to seek God's guidance for the tasks at hand. For many modern-day Christians the forty days of Lent provide an opportunity to bring that sacred time into their lives, to be particularly aware of being in Christ's presence, and to seek God's guidance for the living of these days.

Try to imagine what it must have been like for the disciples during those forty days. They must have felt as if they were being given a second chance with Jesus. He had been taken from them once; they were not going to waste this second opportunity to learn from him. Surely they wanted to make every minute with Jesus count; surely they hung on his every word. According to Acts, the lessons that the risen Christ taught were the same lessons he taught during his earthly ministry: lessons of the kingdom of God (v. 3).

In their three years of traveling with Jesus, the disciples had often misunderstood Jesus' teaching. Therefore, it is not too surprising that once again they misunderstood when Jesus taught about the kingdom of God. For the disciples, a concept of the kingdom of God was deeply ingrained in their thinking. For many years the expectation of the Jewish people had been that the Messiah would come and establish God's kingdom on earth. The messianic promises of the Old Testament prophets would be fulfilled. God's promise to create a new heaven and a new earth and a New Jerusalem (Isa. 65:17–25) would be complete. In the time of Jesus, the Jewish people were under the rule of Rome, and they lived with the constant hope that soon their nation would be liberated. As Jesus taught about the kingdom of God, the disciples assumed he was announcing that this time of fulfillment was about to come to pass. "Is this the time when you will restore the kingdom to Israel?" they ask (Acts 1:6).

 Want to Know More?

About the passion and resurrection of Jesus? See Alyce M. McKenzie, *Matthew*, Interpretation Bible Studies (Louisville, Ky.: Geneva Press, 1998), 83–99, and Richard I. Deibert, *Mark*, Interpretation Bible Studies (Louisville, Ky.: Geneva Press, 1999), 91–120.

About the kingdom of God? See Shirley C. Guthrie, *Christian Doctrine*, revised edition (Louisville, Ky.: Westminster John Knox Press, 1994), 275–87, and Robert H. Stein, *The Method and Message of Jesus' Teachings*, revised edition (Louisville, Ky.: Westminster John Knox Press, 1994), 60–81.

About the messianic expectations? See Celia Brewer Marshall, *A Guide through the New Testament* (Louisville, Ky.: Westminster John Knox Press, 1994), 33.

Their question was understandable but misguided. Jesus had another kind of kingdom in mind. He responded to the disciples' question by affirming that the timing for the fulfillment of God's earthly kingdom was known only to God. Again they were reminded that ultimate sovereignty belongs to God. The timing for the fulfillment of God's kingdom was not the disciples' concern; how to live in the meantime was their concern, so Jesus made a promise: "You will be baptized with the Holy Spirit not many days from now" (Acts 1:5). Jesus was telling about a kingdom empowered by the Holy Spirit. It would be another ten days, the Day of Pentecost, before it would become clear to the disciples exactly what Jesus

"The words of Jesus however have yet another implication. In laying down the course of the Christian mission from Jerusalem to the 'end of the earth,' they also prescribe the content of Acts: the progress of the gospel from Jerusalem to Rome."— Ernst Haenchen, *The Acts of the Apostles: A Commentary* (Philadelphia: Westminster Press, 1971), 144.

meant. The rest of the book of Acts tells of how the disciples gradually came to understand what it meant to live toward this new kingdom of God.

The Ascension of Jesus

The disciples must have hoped that these forty days would stretch to fifty . . . sixty . . . on and on. But when the time was right, Jesus departed again—this time it was not death, but ascension into heaven. As the disciples watched, Jesus was lifted up (Acts 1:9).

For many people today, the account of the ascension of Jesus seems out of sync with our more scientific, sophisticated worldview. It was all right for the disciples with their primitive idea of a three-story universe, but we know that heaven is not "up"—as if someone could hop a ride on the space shuttle and climb higher and higher until finally reaching heaven. Nevertheless, the ascension of Jesus is one of the central tenets of our faith; we say it when we repeat the Apostles' Creed— "He ascended into heaven."

What are we saying when we affirm a belief in the ascension of Jesus? We are affirming that Jesus who died and was raised from the dead now sits at the right hand of God. The resurrection of Jesus brought the good news that death is not the last word. Easter proved that the power of God to give life is greater than the power of death. The ascension of Jesus takes that good news one step farther by affirming that Christ who died and was raised has been given the place of honor by God and now is where he rightfully belongs—on the heavenly throne. "Crown him with many crowns, the Lamb upon his throne."

The ascension of Jesus is God's final confirmation of Jesus. The one whose birth was signaled by a star and announced by the heavenly host, whose baptism was noted by a voice from heaven, now receives God's final sign of approval. Now Jesus sits at the right hand of God. The ascension of Jesus is not about direction—that Jesus is going "up." Rather it is that Jesus is returning to God from whom he had come in his birth at Bethlehem. Jesus has now come full circle— he was in the form of God, but gave up his God-ness in order to become a human being, to live the life of a servant. And now God has exalted him and given him the name that is above every name (Phil. 2:5–11).

The Handoff

But there's more. The significance of the ascension was not just what it meant to Jesus; it also meant something to Jesus' disciples. The disciples stood watching as Jesus disappeared into the clouds. They didn't want to look away; they kept their eyes fixed on that point as long as they could. They stood with their necks stretched upward and their eyes squinting into the sky. Suddenly two men in white robes (v. 11) joined them and said, "Why do you stand here looking up toward heaven?" What happened next would be crucial. Would the disciples do as they had done before? Would they conclude that this "Jesus thing" was all over and they may as well go back to fishing? Or would they accept the challenge of continuing the work that Jesus had begun? To accept that challenge would take them into some new and uncertain waters. Could they do it? It's no wonder they lingered gazing up into the sky. With the ascension of Jesus into heaven, the responsibility for spreading God's word rested squarely on the shoulders of Jesus' followers—Jesus' denying, doubting, misunderstanding, fearful disciples!

> " 'Why do you stand looking into heaven?' There is work to be done; let the church be about the work in the meantime, secure in the promise that Jesus who was so dramatically taken from his disciples shall return to them in the same way."—William H. Willimon, *Acts*, Interpretation, 20.

The ascension was the handoff. It's like the son who has been working in his father's business and one day the father comes to the store and says, "Son, I'm not going to be coming in as much any more; you can handle things here." It was a day the son knew was coming, but could he handle it? Could he keep up the things that his father had begun?

Here Jesus is making the handoff to the disciples. The story is told that on ascending into heaven, Jesus went to God the Creator to give a report about his time on earth. All the angels and archangels gathered around to hear what Jesus had to say about his experiences among the women and men walking the earth. Jesus told about preaching and teaching; he told about how he had tried to tell the world about God's great love. He said that there were some people who seemed to be persuaded and followed him around as he traveled from place to place. He also told about his crucifixion and death. He told about denial and betrayal and disciples running away in fear. And when he came to the part about how he had entrusted to his followers the responsibility to spread the good news of God's love, to continue to tell the story, one of the angels gasped and said, "O, but Jesus, what if they fail?" And Jesus replied, "I have no other plan."

This was the critical moment if the disciples were to fulfill Jesus' plan. The disciples understood that if the work of Jesus was to go on, it would be up to them to do it. The body of Christ on earth was no longer Jesus' physical body, but the corporate body of believers. This remains true about believers today. Teresa of Avila (1515–1582) wrote:

> Christ has no body now on earth but yours, no hands but yours, no feet but yours; yours are the eyes through which is to look out Christ's compassion to the world. Yours are the feet with which he is to go about doing good, yours are the hands with which he is to bless . . . now. (As cited in Harvey, 206)

The good news is that with the handoff comes the reassuring knowledge that we know the one who sits at the right hand of God . . . and he knows us! In those times of life when all we can see is the muck and mire of daily existence, and when it seems that all life has to offer is one problem after another, we can lift our eyes. To believe in the ascension of Jesus is to believe that the One who is truly in charge of all life is God, the Creator, Redeemer, and Sustainer of life.

For those early Christians, as they undertook the mission to continue to spread the good news of Jesus, there must have been many times when they felt at their wits' end and overwhelmed by the challenges at hand. In those times, it must have been great comfort to remind themselves that they knew—and were known by—the one who was sitting at the right hand of God. As it was for those early Christians, it is still so for us.

> "In Jesus' final statement to his apostles he promises that they *will receive power* —not to rule, but to witness."—Paul W. Walaskay, *Acts*, Westminster Bible Companion, 28.

Don't Just Stand There!

If the disciples were to undertake this awesome task, what were they to do? What would they do next? They went back to Jerusalem and waited (v. 12)! Jesus had promised that they would be filled with the power of the Holy Spirit, and so they waited.

Waiting is not our strong suit. In our fast-food, high-speed, "don't just sit there, do something" age, waiting is not something we do well. Waiting is too passive; we prefer to be active, taking charge. Waiting is the acknowledgment that we are not in control. William Willimon says, "Our waiting implies that the things which need doing in the world are beyond our ability to accomplish solely by our own effort. . . . Some other empowerment is needed" (Willimon, 21).

The disciples knew that without some help they could not undertake the task of being Christ's witnesses "in Jerusalem, in all Judea and Samaria, and to the ends of the earth" (v. 8), so they waited for that power to come. But their waiting was not an empty time. It was a time filled with prayer (v. 14). Some people might argue that they could have spent their time more productively. They could have taken charge—planning, organizing, and getting things in order. Instead, they prayed. For the disciples at that critical moment, prayer was the only right use of their time.

"You will be my witnesses in Jerusalem."

Prayer served as a regular reminder of God's presence and power in their lives. Prayer was the reminder that it was God's will, not their own, which they were seeking to do.

That is a lesson we all need to learn. How often do we set out on some well-intentioned project without first getting our proper bearings? As the needle in a compass always points to the magnetic north pole, so prayer is the pointer that always orients us in the right direction.

The Thirteenth Disciple

The disciples waited and prayed for God's guidance. As we read this account in Acts and try to imagine what it must have felt like to be in the shoes of the disciples, we can almost hear one of them. "I'm not exactly sure what we are supposed to do next, but I do know there are supposed to be twelve of us doing it. Jesus picked twelve, and now that Judas has died his gory death, we're down to eleven. We need someone else." So Peter, never one to keep his thoughts to himself, proposed that a replacement for Judas be found. He suggested the criterion—it should be someone who had been with Jesus from the beginning. Apparently the other disciples agreed, and two persons made the

"Prayer keeps our hearts chasing after God's heart. It's how we bother God, and how God bothers us back."—Barbara Brown Taylor, "Bothering God," *Christian Century*, March 24–31, 1999, p. 356.

short list—Joseph called Barsabbas and Matthias. They cast lots, and Matthias was chosen.

On one level this seems like a rather insignificant event—just another election to fill an empty slot on a board. But on another level this is an act of genuine faithfulness. The disciples had just been given the impossible task of being witnesses in Jerusalem, Judea and Samaria, and to the ends of the earth. It must have seemed too much for them to do. Surely some entertained the possibility of giving up and going fishing. But they did not do that. They may not have known all that was expected of them, but they did know that if they were going to make any headway, they would need their full complement. Whenever their next step would become clear to them, they wanted to be ready.

> **How were tough decisions made?**
>
> "It may seem strange to us that the method was that of casting lots. But amongst the Jews it was a natural thing to do because all the offices and duties in the Temple were settled that way. The names of the candidates were written on stones; the stones were put into a vessel and the vessel was shaken until one stone fell out; and he whose name was on that stone was elected to office."—William Barclay, *Acts*, Daily Study Bible, 17.

And with that, the stage was set. Now all they were missing was guidance, direction, and power to do the work. For that we proceed on into the book of Acts.

? Questions for Reflection

1. This unit began by mentioning the period of time of 40 days, and described it as "sacred time." What do you think is meant by the phrase "sacred time?" When are your sacred times? What makes them sacred?

2. At the ascension, the apostles are left standing and looking up at the sky. They are chastised for just standing around. Contrast this episode with the story of Mary and Martha in Luke 10:38–42. How should Christians behave—should they be still or be active? Why do you think so?

3. This early community is described as constantly devoted to prayer (v. 14). What are the things you are devoted to? What is the role of prayer in your life? What are the things you pray for?

4. To complete their group, the apostles cast lots to add another. How do you respond to that selection process? How high is your confidence in the validity of that choice? How are leaders chosen in church today?

2 Acts 2:1-42

Pentecost

Price Gwynn, former moderator of the Presbyterian Church (U.S.A.), tells a story about an experience he had while moderator. Part of his responsibility was to represent the denomination at various church assemblies all over the world. On this particular occasion, he was on the island of Cyprus and was invited to speak at an Eastern Orthodox church. It was highly unusual for a Western Christian to be asked to speak. In fact, the priest who issued the invitation had been severely criticized by his colleagues for asking Price Gwynn to speak. But Moderator Gwynn was there. The worship service that day included the celebration of the sacrament of the Lord's Supper. In that tradition, the method for receiving Communion is somewhat different from what is done in most American churches. Rather than the more familiar common cup, they had what might be called the "common spoon." To prepare the elements, the priest took a large clay pot, poured in the wine and then added big chunks of the bread, making a wine/bread mush. To take Communion, one by one the worshipers would come forward, and the priest, using a large silver spoon, would spoon out some of the mush into the mouth of the communicant. Gwynn watched as the people came forward and time and again the spoon was dipped from bowl to mouth. Among the communicants were people from all walks of life: there were rich people, poor people, people with black teeth, some with no teeth. One by one they took their spoonful of the Communion elements.

As the people were coming forward for communion, Gwynn leaned over to his traveling companion, an Egyptian pastor, and told him that he would not be taking Communion. The pastor,

14

sensing his squeamishness, asked, "Are your reasons theological?" The moderator replied, "No; they are sanitary." The whispered conversation continued as the pastor said that if he refused to take Communion, this Orthodox priest would be ridiculed and criticized even more. So, having earlier declined for sanitary reasons, now for theological reasons Moderator Gwynn took his place in line and received Communion.

How did he do that? Where did he get the power to override all his natural instincts to take his place with those who were coming to partake of this unsanitary version of the Supper of the Lamb? The answer is found in the passage that is before us.

Another example. In her book, *Tramp for the Lord*, Corrie ten Boom tells about an experience she had during her travels after World War II. During the war, Corrie ten Boom was imprisoned in the Nazi prison camp at Ravensbruck—she and her sister Betsie. There in that camp her sister died in the gas ovens. After the war was over, Corrie ten Boom became an evangelist. She traveled all over the world preaching the gospel, telling about God's powerful, forgiving love. On one such occasion, she was in Germany, and after her sermon she was greeting the people who were in attendance. In the audience was a man who came forward to shake her hand. Suddenly for Corrie ten Boom there was the flash of recognition as she identified the man as one of the prison guards who had stood watch at the doors to the ovens where so many people, including her sister, were killed. As he stood there with his hand outstretched to shake her hand, she said that the memories of that terrible time came flooding over her—the grief, the hardship, the suffering. Here's how she tells what happened next. "I fumbled in my pocketbook rather than take his hand. My blood seemed to freeze. I knew I had to forgive if I wanted to receive God's forgiveness, still I stood there with the coldness clutching my heart." She began to pray. She knew that she could not find the power to forgive, but she could at least raise her hand. Slowly she took his hand, and when she did a rush of genuine forgiveness came over her. She said to him, "I forgive you, brother." As she tells it, "For a long moment we grasped each others' hands, the former guard and the former prisoner. I had never known God's love so intensely as I did then. But even so, I realized it was not my love. I had tried, but I did not have the power" (Ten Boom, 55–57).

How did she do that? What was the source of the power that enabled her to shake the hand and to forgive her former enemy? The answer to that question is found in the passage before us.

Pentecost

This story tells of the first Pentecost. In the forty days after Easter, Jesus continued to appear to his disciples, and he reaffirmed the promise he had made earlier that he would not leave them alone. He said, "You will receive power when the Holy Spirit comes upon you, and you will be my witnesses in Jerusalem, in all Judea and Samaria, and to the ends of the earth" (Acts 1:8). Having made that promise, Jesus departed from them and ascended into heaven. So the disciples waited. Ten days.

"More than one interpretation can be offered for what happened in the upper room at Pentecost. No single formulation can do it justice. We are listening to the account of something strange, beyond the bounds of imagination, miraculous, inscrutable, an origin which, as far as Luke is concerned, was the only way one could 'explain' the existence of the church."—William H. Willimon, *Acts*, Interpretation, 29.

On the Day of Pentecost, the disciples were gathered together in one place when suddenly there was a sound like the rush of a violent wind and then tongues of fire descended upon them. All of them were filled with the Holy Spirit.

Readers familiar with the Jewish traditions will recognize the wind and the fire. In the story of creation, Genesis says that the wind from God swept over the waters at creation (Gen. 1:2). And when Moses went up on Mount Sinai to meet God and receive the Ten Commandments, the mountain was covered with smoke and fire (Ex. 19:16–18). The wind and the fire were signs of the presence of God. Here at Pentecost God was bringing forth a new creation, bringing a new law.

The Pentecost experience recalled God's revelation on Mount Sinai.

This was not the first time that the Holy Spirit had filled a person with power. In the days of the Old Testament prophets, the Holy Spirit would empower the one who would be God's prophet. In those days, the Spirit was particular. Some were filled with the Spirit and some were not. The empowering of the Holy Spirit was rare, and in fact, it was said that it had been many years since God raised up a prophet. But on the Day of Pentecost, the Holy Spirit was not particular, empowering one and skipping over the next. At Pentecost, the Holy Spirit was universal; all received the power of the Spirit.

This was a whole new thing. That Pentecost day, all were filled with the power of the Holy Spirit, just as Jesus has promised. No one was passed over. This was God's new creation. The Holy Spirit was poured out upon all, filling all, empowering all.

Who Was Present There?

It's tempting to skim quickly through the list of various ethnic groups named in 2:9–11. At a glance, Luke appears to be saying that lots of people from all over were present on that first Pentecost—they came from north, south, east, and west. But there is more to this list than mere geography. Thomas G. Long writes,

> This conglomeration of peoples is not only a diverse and pluralistic gathering of tourists, it is also an historically impossible collection of folks. Consider the Medes, for instance. They must have had a rather difficult journey to Jerusalem since they would not only have had to travel several hundred miles, but several hundred years as well, Medes having already disappeared from the canvas of history. (Long, 28)

Why would Luke include in this listing a nation that had passed from the stage of world history? Luke wants his readers to know that when he says that "every nation under heaven" was present there, he meant it. The nations in attendance at Pentecost represented the ends of the earth geographically and historically. The creative power of the Spirit at Pentecost was transforming all people—past, present, and future.

Miraculously, in this geographically and historically diverse gathering, people communicated with one another. Do not get mired down in trying to figure out how it happened. It was not like being at the United Nations, where the delegates don earphones for simultaneous translations. It was not like the Star Trek Universal Translator, which can instantly translate any spoken word. Was it the tongues of the speakers that were affected or the ears of the hearers? Luke leaves the matter foggy so that we will

> "We are hearing a story about the irruption of the Spirit into the community and the first fruit of the Spirit—the gift of proclamation."—William H. Willimon, *Acts*, Interpretation, 30.

not get caught up in that kind of mechanistic mess. The miracle of communication was itself a gift of the Holy Spirit.

Last year my wife and I worshiped at a Roman Catholic mass at the Duomo, the Cathedral of Santa Maria, in Florence, Italy. The familiar orange-tiled roof of the dome rises 300 feet above the ground and is Florence's most famous landmark. The Duomo is a huge cathedral—fourth largest in the world, according to the guidebooks. The ceiling of the dome is covered with frescoes depicting the last judgment; the floors are intricate multicolored inlaid marble. There is gold everywhere; masterpieces of art and sculpture are in every corner. As we arrived for worship, the organ filled the magnificent building with music.

At first look, one could say that for my wife and me this was a totally foreign and strange environment—a Roman Catholic mass, in Italian, in a place totally unlike where we are accustomed to worship. However, it was not that way at all. Even though we did not speak the language, we could follow along in the service, because we brought to that experience of worship our own experiences of worship in other times and places and thus were able to find common ground. The Lord's Prayer and some of the responses in the liturgy were familiar, even though they were in another language. Even though they were speaking in their own language, it was as if we were hearing in our own language—because, at some deep level, all people share a hunger for and an expression of faith.

> "The Holy Spirit is a great equalizer."—Kathleen Norris, *Amazing Grace: A Vocabulary of Faith* (New York: Riverhead Books, 1998), 348.

Perhaps that was what happened at Pentecost. By the power of the Holy Spirit, each person was touched in a fundamental way. The Spirit addressed issues and needs so deeply felt that each person understood regardless of the language that was being spoken.

Peter's Sermon

This miraculous communication evoked questions ("What does this mean?") and snide remarks ("They've been drinking"). The comments of the people called for some response from the disciples. We are surprised when we see the one who rose to speak. It is Peter. Although Peter had spoken briefly in Acts 1, the lingering memory of Peter is of his repeated failures at the time of Jesus' crucifixion. This was the same Peter who only weeks before had been afraid to speak even to a servant girl (Luke 22:56–57). This was the same Peter who three times denied knowing Jesus. This was the same Peter whose failures left him weeping bitterly. But now, that same Peter is standing before the very people who had arrested, tried, and crucified Jesus, declaring his faith in Jesus. How did he do that? Where did he find the power?

Peter's sermon itself is evidence of the power of the Holy Spirit to transform a person. As William Willimon says, "In Acts 2:1–4 the Spirit has breathed life into a once cowardly disciple and created a new man who now has the gift of bold speech" (Willimon, 32).

Peter boldly declares that the crucified and risen Christ is the fulfillment of the Old Testament prophecies and promises. Then he urges his hearers, "Repent, and be baptized every one of you in the name of Jesus Christ so that your sins may be forgiven; and you will receive the gift of the Holy Spirit." This empowering by the Holy Spirit is available to everyone—"for you, for your children, and for all who are far away" (vv. 38–39).

> "When the Spirit comes . . . the world-wide mission starts at full gallop, and the gospel is preached to representatives 'from every nation under heaven' no less!"—James D. G. Dunn, *Baptism in the Holy Spirit* (Philadelphia: Westminster Press, 1977), 49.

A word needs to be said about verse 40. Most of our various English translations say something like "Save yourselves . . . ," which is a blurring of the intention of the Greek. A better rendering might be "Let yourselves be saved. . . ." Peter is certain that salvation itself is a gift of the Holy Spirit, and not a human work. The truth is that we cannot save ourselves. But we can be saved by the grace of God and the redeeming love of Christ and the power of the Holy Spirit.

Power

Reading this story, we see clearly that the power of the Holy Spirit enabled the disciples to do two things. First, it enabled them to speak. This sermon by Peter is the first of many speeches in Acts in which the disciples boldly witness to their faith in Jesus in all sorts of circumstances. The same disciples who only weeks before were running in fear, denying, doubting were now standing up boldly declaring their faith in the crucified and

> "The Spirit is the power which enables the church to 'go public' with its good news, to attract a crowd and . . . to have something to say worth hearing."—William H. Willimon, *Acts*, Interpretation, 33.

risen Christ. How did they do that? Where did they find that power? It was certainly not drawn from their own ability. It was the Holy Spirit who gave them the words to speak and the courage to speak them.

> "The Spirit of God that moved across the face of the deep and created the heavens and the earth, that overshadowed Mary's flesh and brought forth Jesus, that descended upon Jesus at his baptism, announcing his sonship and anointing his mission, now let itself loose upon the church."—H. Stephen Shoemaker, *God-Stories* (Valley Forge, Pa.: Judson Press, 1998), 293.

It has been that way ever since. Since the day of Pentecost believers, filled with the Holy Spirit, have told and retold the story of Jesus. It was the power of the Spirit that enabled Price Gwynn to join with his brothers and sisters to share the sacramental meal. It was the power of the Holy Spirit that enabled Corrie Ten Boom to experience God's forgiving love both for herself and for her former enemy. Every believer has been given that power.

Want to Know More?

About the Lord's Supper? See William Barclay, *The Lord's Supper* (Philadelphia: Westminster Press, 1982), and Markus Barth, *Rediscovering the Lord's Supper* (Atlanta: John Knox Press, 1988).

About Pentecost? See J. G. Davies, ed., *The New Westminster Dictionary of Liturgy and Worship* (Philadelphia: Westminster Press, 1986), 429–30 and James D. G. Dunn, *Baptism in the Holy Spirit* (Philadelphia: Westminster Press, 1977), 38–54.

About speaking in tongues? See Frank Stagg, E. Glenn Hinson, and Wayne E. Oates, *Glossolalia: Tongue Speaking in Biblical, Historical, and Psychological Perspective* (Nashville: Abingdon Press, 1967), and Watson E. Mills, *Speaking in Tongues: A Guide to Research on Glossolalia* (Grand Rapids: Wm. B. Eerdmans Publishing Co., 1986).

The second effect of this empowering by the Holy Spirit is recounted in Acts 2:42–47. It says that the followers of Jesus "were together and had all things in common; they would sell their possessions and goods and distribute the proceeds to all, as any had need" (vv. 44–45). By the power of the Holy Spirit, believers began to think about *things* in a new way, to see that the common good of the community was more important than their own individual wants and needs. Can there be a more remarkable evidence of the Holy Spirit's transforming power? To build a community devoted to one another, to create hearts that love, to inspire persons to sacrifice self for the larger good—these are genuine marks of a new life.

Are those marks seen in the church today? To what degree are the members of your church "devoted to one another"? Can you think of ways that this gift of the Spirit can be more fully experienced in your community of faith?

The power that transformed those early Christians is still at work among us. It's been that way for two millennia now, as believers have found the power to do the impossible—to forgive the unforgivable, to love the unlovable, to give up their own rights in order to give rights to others. How can they do that? Certainly it is not by their own power. It could only be by the power of God's Spirit at work in the world.

? Questions for Reflection

1. This unit speaks about being empowered by the Spirit to do extraordinary things, and examples were given of instances of the Spirit's power. What are evidences of the presence of God's Spirit?
2. Some have observed that in Acts geographic references sometimes also have a theological intent. What are some examples you have noticed in Acts so far?
3. Verses 38–39 link baptism with both forgiveness and receipt of the Holy Spirit. How are these three related? Must one be baptized to be forgiven? Why or why not?
4. Peter argues that Jesus is the fulfillment of Old Testament expectations. What is convincing about his argument? Why?

3 Acts 4:32–5:11

Life (and Death) in the Early Christian Community

Flannery O'Connor wrote, "Our beliefs are not what we see; they are the light by which we see" (cited in an article by H. Richard Niebuhr, 207ff.). For the new Christians their belief in the resurrection of Jesus gave them a completely new light by which to look at all of life. Christianity has been compared to a store window in which someone has sneaked in and switched around all the price tags. The things that had been thought of as valuable are no longer all that valuable, and the things that had been seen as being of little value were now priceless. The light of the resurrection of Jesus did just that, shining a new light on every aspect of life. All of the assumptions they had about life and death were overturned, and they began to look at things in a whole new way. Their new way of thinking changed their perceptions about the momentous events of life, but it also filtered down so that it affected even their daily lives. After the "big" events of the first three chapters of Acts—the ascension of Jesus, Pentecost, miracles done by the apostles—this description of daily life in the Christian community seems rather ordinary by comparison. However, the crucifixion, resurrection, and ascension of Jesus changed everything—even the mundane activities of daily life. The early church took some brave steps.

> "It is the community's business to speak the word with boldness in the midst of the mighty acts of God."—William H. Willimon, *Acts*, Interpretation, 50.

There is a scene in Peter Shaffer's play *Equus*, in which the father of a teenage boy who is undergoing psychotherapy is talking to his son's psychiatrist. The boy has committed a series of violent acts. The father says, "I'm an atheist, and I don't mind admitting it. If you want my opinion, it's the Bible that responsible for all this." When the psy-

22

chiatrist asks him to explain, the father responds, "Well, look at it yourself. A boy spends night after night having this stuff read into him: an innocent man tortured to death—thorns driven into his head—nails into his hands—a spear pierced through the ribs. It can mark anyone for life, that sort of thing" (Shaffer, 34).

The crucifixion of Jesus can indeed "mark" a person. Jesus' crucifixion—and resurrection and ascension!—marked the disciples forever. As Acts gives us a picture of life together in that early Christian community, it is clear that attention to the resurrection of Jesus was at the center. "With great power the apostles gave their testimony to the resurrection of the Lord Jesus, and great grace was upon them all" (v. 33). The resurrection of Jesus completely changed things. It changed the way they thought about their life in community, and it changed the way they thought about their possessions, security, money. Their belief in the resurrection forced them to give up on the old way of looking at life and death, and to begin to see things in a whole new way. William Willimon has written,

> The most eloquent testimony to the reality of the resurrection is not an empty tomb or a well-orchestrated pageant on Easter Sunday but rather a group of people whose life together is so radically different, so completely changed from the way the world builds community, that there can be no explanation other than that something decisive has happened in history. (Willimon, 51)

Here in Acts 4, we see how this belief in the resurrection of Jesus caused the disciples and the early Christians to think in a new way about what it meant to live together.

Life Together

"The whole group of those who believed were of one heart and soul" (v. 32). When Luke wrote Acts, several years had passed since these early days of the church. In the intervening years, the church had experienced no small amount of upheaval. There had been the considerable debate about whether or not to allow Gentiles into the body of believers. (The church's response to this question takes up much of the remainder of Acts.) From Paul's letters we learn that there had been debates over how to observe the Lord's Supper (1 Corinthians 11), over the meaning of spiritual gifts (1 Corinthians 12), as well as other issues. By the time Luke sat down to write Acts, the church had been forced to work its way through a number of conflicts. Perhaps it was those conflicts that made Luke describe those earliest days of the Christian community with such fondness. Luke was looking back to "the good old days."

Pastors who have worked as new church developers starting new congregations often talk about those earliest days of the new congregation with this kind of Lukan wistfulness. They say that in the early days so much energy is required to get a church up and running that there is no energy left for squabbling with each other. Once the new church is established and the issues of church life move from basic survival to expansion and growth, then they discover the luxury of disagreeing. Perhaps it was this same phenomenon that Luke was experiencing as he looked back to the earliest days of the church.

Thomas G. Long has observed that one often finds similar language when reading the history of a local congregation. The history of First Presbyterian Church of Monroe, North Carolina (the church I serve as pastor) was written on the occasion of its 100th anniversary in 1973. The historian looks back to the early 1900s, when the members undertook the bold step of building a new sanctuary, and states with pride that it was accomplished because "all the members worked in harmony, looking to the same end and laboring with a spirit of brotherly (sic) love." Perhaps this historian had endured enough church squabbles to look back to those days with such nostalgia. Is that kind of writing just nostalgia? Long suggests that it is a "description of the church's past in terms of its best hopes for the future . . . in terms of where the church trusts that its ministry and its Lord are taking it" (Long, 30).

Not a Needy Person among Them

"The power which broke the bonds of death on Easter, shattered the divisions of speech at Pentecost, and empowered one who was lame now releases the tight grip of private property."—William H. Willimon, Acts, Interpretation, 53.

As Luke looks back to those earliest days of the church, he says, "There was not a needy person among them" (vv. 32–34). Through the ages a characteristic of the Christian community has been a concern for the poor and generosity in giving. However, many people find the generosity of Christians hard to comprehend. In the third century, the popular Roman writer Lucian wrote about the behavior he observed among the Christians of his day. What he saw the Christians doing amazed him. He talked about "their absurd generosity and their sacrificial concern for others whom they didn't even know by name" (from *The Death of Peregrinus,* by Lucian of Samosata). It simply didn't make any sense to him that people would be willing to give of themselves for others. We should not be surprised that Lucian might feel this way. Generosity, concern for others, is not something that comes naturally. It happens only because people choose to be that way. So why would people be willing to act in such a way? Why would someone choose to be generous, to be concerned for others? In the early church it was because they were living in response to the resurrection of Jesus. "With great power the apostles gave their testimony to the resurrection of the Lord Jesus." Acts doesn't tell us exactly what the apostles said, so we can only surmise. As people heard the apostles telling about God's love made known in the life, death, and resurrection of Jesus, they found their hearts warmed and their minds opened to the possibility that perhaps there might be a place for them among the followers of Jesus. It was their experience of the power of the risen Christ that had brought them into the company of the believers, and it was that same experience of the power of the risen Christ that made them reach out to others.

"Everything they owned was held in common" (v. 32). For twentieth-century Western Christians, this sentence grates like fingers on a chalkboard. It irritates, even angers. It sounds like communism! Indeed, it is communism—communism in its purest form. The sentence grates on us because it is so contrary to the values of individualism and self-determination that pervade our society. In their insightful study titled *Habits of the Heart: Individualism and Commitment in American Life,* sociologist Robert Bellah and his

> "The sharing of material possessions with one another was an outward manifestation of a deeper spiritual unity."—Charles H. Talbert, Acts, Knox Preaching Guides (Atlanta: John Knox Press, 1984), 23.

colleagues analyze the conflict between our fierce individualism and our need for community. "Individualism lies at the very core of American culture" (Bellah, 142). They observe that we value individualism over community. Our heroes and role models are those who by hard work and determination have "made it." And "making it" is generally measured in material success. We live in a society that accepts the wide economic disparity between rich and poor as simply the way things are. In such a society, the idea that one would sacrifice self-gain for the good of the larger community seems foreign.

By contrast to our Western notion that values individualism, there are societies that understand that more valuable than the individual is the whole. T. R. Reid's book on his experiences living in Japan (*Confucius Lives Next Door: What Living in the East Teaches Us about Living in the West*) tells some of the lessons he learned during the years he lived in Tokyo. One of the lessons came from his next-door neighbor, Matsuda-san. Reid says that when he looked at his neighborhood, he saw "a drab collection of small cement houses lining narrow, busy streets." But when Matsuda-san looked at that same neighborhood, he saw a community; he saw people. In that Asian way of looking at things, to refuse to accept one's place in and responsibility to the larger group is selfishness (Reid, 74–75).

> Responsibility for each other is more intricate than we commonly imagine. Maria Harris writes, "We belong to a species where one act of compassion has ramifications for everyone . . . where one act of cruelty touches us all."—*Proclaim Jubilee: A Spirituality for the Twenty-first Century* (Louisville, Ky.: Westminster John Knox Press, 1996), 8–9.

Those early Christians knew that there could be no real community when people in a position to alleviate the needs of others refuse to do so. As long as there were people in need the community was not whole.

Barnabas

The Christian church was growing, and people from all economic levels were coming in. There were the well-to-do, and there were those whose resources were limited. For some of the members of the church, life was hard and even the basic necessities of life were scarce. It was a problem that the church had to address. Barnabas was the one who set the example. He sold a piece of property and gave the money from the sale to the church. Soon others followed his example. Through their generosity a fund was set up to help the poor, the widows and orphans. It started with Barnabas, whose name means "son of encouragement." What an admirable nickname!

Present-day Cyprus, the homeland of Barnabas.

Barnabas is not a particularly well-known character of the New Testament, certainly not like Peter and Paul, but one could argue that he was every bit as influential as they were in the growth and expansion of the Christian church. He did it in a quiet way with gentle words of encouragement.

Here in Acts 4 is not the only place Barnabas is mentioned. He appears again in 9:26–27. Saul of Tarsus, later known as Paul, had been converted to Christianity, but some of the apostles had a difficult time accepting Saul. Previously Saul had devoted his life to persecuting Christians, and many people were suspicious of Saul's supposed miraculous conversion. What Saul needed was someone who would stand up for him, and that person was Barnabas. Barnabas talked to Saul, became convinced of his sincerity, and took him to meet with the apostles.

We see Barnabas again in 11:19–26. Word had come to the church in Jerusalem that the believers in Antioch were preaching the gospel to Gentiles. In Jerusalem, where Christians were being persecuted, there was fear of the Gentiles. The Jerusalem Christians were wary of opening the church to Gentiles as was happening in Antioch.

Want to Know More?

About Paul's first letter to the Corinthians? See Bruce N. Fisk, *First Corinthians*, Interpretation Bible Studies (Louisville, Ky.: Geneva Press, 2000).

About biblical concern for the poor and needy? For a good beginning, see James Limburg, *The Prophets and the Powerless* (Atlanta: John Knox Press, 1977), 25–38. See also Robert McAfee Brown, *Unexpected News: Reading the Bible with Third World Eyes* (Philadelphia: Westminster Press, 1984).

So they sent Barnabas to investigate. That proved to be a very good choice. Barnabas, the "son of encouragement," went to Antioch, saw that indeed God's grace was being given to Jews and Gentiles alike, and he gave his approval for the spread of the gospel among Gentiles. Barnabas stayed on in Antioch to help. While there in Antioch, Barnabas sent for Saul and invited him to join in their work.

Barnabas was not done yet. Encouraged by the success in Antioch, Barnabas returned to Jerusalem to argue that more missionary work should be undertaken. Barnabas, Paul, and John Mark were commissioned and sent off as missionaries. This first missionary journey is recounted in Acts 13–15.

Barnabas, this son of encouragement, is a good model for every Christian. Barnabas seemed to look for the best in a person and was always there with an encouraging word.

A few years ago a three-on-three basketball tournament was being televised. It was the finals, and the two teams were made up of players who were tall and strong; they could run and shoot; they had all the good basketball moves. But here they were playing in obscurity while other, no more talented, players were in the NBA making huge salaries. One of the announcers was Dominique Wilkins, an NBA star, and during one of the breaks in the action, the other announcer asked Dominique what was the difference between the players in this three-on-three tournament and those in the NBA. Dominique said, "Nothing really, except that they probably didn't have the people to help them and encourage them to keep going through the hard times."

Barnabas, the son of encouragement, may not have had the strong personality of Peter or the varied gifts of Paul, but he used the gifts he had. Luke describes him like this: "a good man, full of the Holy Spirit and faith."

Ananias and Sapphira

On the heels of this story about Barnabas's encouraging generosity comes the troubling story of Ananias and Sapphira. Apparently inspired by the example of Barnabas, Ananias and Sapphira followed suit . . . almost. They too sold some property and gave proceeds from the sale to the apostles. However, they held back a portion for themselves, and with that decision, things turned sour. Before their story was done, they had both fallen dead out of shame, guilt, or fear.

> "The cost of not confronting our deceit over possessions is high—nothing less than the very death of our life together."—William H. Willimon, *Acts*, Interpretation, 54.

What did they do that was so bad? They did not cheat anyone or steal from anyone or do anything to harm another person. Their sin was that they lied to the community—and thus to God—about their possessions. The problem was not with what they gave, but with *what they held on to*. It's an issue that every Christian must consider seriously. A large portion of Jesus' teaching concerns possessions and money. Recall Jesus' familiar words in the Sermon on the Mount: "Where your treasure is, there your heart will be also" (Matt. 6:21), and "You cannot serve God and wealth" (Matt. 6:24). Or consider Jesus' warning to the rich in Luke 6:24–25. Luke

> "Lying to God is like sawing the branch you're sitting on. The better you do it, the harder you fall."—Frederick Buechner, *Peculiar Treasures: A Biblical Who's Who* (New York: Harper & Row, 1979), 12.

18:18–25 tells of Jesus' encounter with the rich young ruler. Jesus was well aware that the way people thought about possessions was a potential stumbling block of faith.

How we treat our possessions is an indicator of what we believe about God. Do we believe that God's promise to provide for us can be trusted, or do we believe we must provide for ourselves? It takes a bold step of faith to trust that God's promises are true. Ananias and Sapphira were unable to take that step. In commenting on this story of Ananias and Sapphira, Paul Walaskay says,

> This story reminds us that all we have . . . belongs to God. . . . Many of us mistakenly assume that the paycheck is compensation *to us* for our labors. Rather, we are being compensated for God's gracious gifts of life, energy, strength, intellect, creativity, and talent. That paycheck is God's. We take out our living allowance, which is usually quite generous, and share (not "give") the rest with those in need. Lying about the source of our resources is self-deceit and arrogance. (Walaskay, 62)

To return to the opening thought from Flannery O'Connor, what is the light by which you see? For those early Christians, the resurrection of Christ shed a new light. Life together in that community of believers brought unity and encouragement, it brought challenges, and it brought a new way of living. That's what the resurrection of Jesus did in the first century. Will the same thing be said about the church in the twenty-first century?

? Questions for Reflection

1. This unit speaks about the "marks" of a Christian. What are the distinguishing features or marks of a disciple?
2. If you were to read the history of your local congregation, what might you find? What would be the "high" points and the "low" points in that history? Often a church will have a charter with a statement of vision or mission. If your church was started with such a statement, what was it? How has the church lived up to that statement?
3. The story of Barnabas is contrasted with that of Ananias and Sapphira. What are the lessons of these stories? (Notice the juxtaposition of the phrases "great grace was upon them all" in 4:32 and "great fear seized them all" in 5:5 and 5:11.) How do you respond to the demise of Ananias and Sapphira? In your opinion,

are there parallel ways that God acts with us today? Why or why not?

4. The word "heart" appears several times in this passage. If you have time, look up this term in a good Bible dictionary. Using a concordance, check the uses in both Luke and Acts. What did the ancients understand about the heart? What is the function and importance of the heart? What part does one's heart play in one's faith relationship with God?

4

The Conversion of Saul

We come today to a story we know too well: Saul's conversion on the road to Damascus. Who knows how many primary department Sunday school teachers have used the familiar pictures or the flannelgraph with its little cloth cutouts to retell this story? We can vividly imagine the bright noonday light that blinded Saul and drove him to his knees. We can visualize the kneeling Saul looking upward as the voice from heaven calls, "Saul, Saul." And we can see Saul's confused friends, leading blind Saul into the city. What Christian has not heard the story of Saul's dramatic conversion?

> "We must try as far as we can to enter into Paul's mind. When we do, we will see that this is not a sudden conversion but a sudden surrender."—William Barclay, *Acts, Daily Study Bible*, 70.

It is no wonder that we know this story so well. It is told three times in Acts (chaps. 9, 22, and 26). William Willimon notes, "Only an event of the greatest importance would merit such repetition by an author whose hallmark is brevity and concision" (p. 74).

The story of Saul's conversion has become the conversion experience by which all conversion experiences are measured. Many conservative Christians question whether someone who cannot name the date and hour that he or she was "saved" is really a Christian. And often, people who have not had this dramatic, strike-you-blind, knock-you-down kind of experience are made to feel spiritually inadequate. A "road to Damascus experience" has become the way to describe a *real* conversion.

It's because we know this story so well and have attached so much baggage to it that it deserves a closer look.

The Scriptural Neighborhood

I'm one of those people who likes maps. If I am going on a trip, I like to study the map so that I can know where I am. I like to know about the surroundings of the place I will be visiting—is it rolling hills, mountains, desert? Are there sights nearby that I don't want to miss? I like to know where I am in relation to other familiar landmarks. Is it near the ocean? What's the climate like? Knowing the surroundings makes me a more informed and knowledgeable traveler.

The same principle applies to our reading of the Bible. Sometimes when we are looking at a particular passage, we don't take the time to step back and look at the larger context—to study the surroundings. And often knowing something about the surroundings adds to the meaning of a particular block of scripture. That is particularly true of this familiar passage. So before we look specifically at Acts 9:1–19, we should do some exploring, roam around in the surrounding chapters and verses. Let's get a feel for the landscape, the terrain in which this story is located.

Back in chapter 1 of Acts, the disciples of Jesus are commissioned to be Christ's witnesses in "Judea and Samaria, and to the ends of the earth" (1:8). Think of this like concentric circles. Judea was at the center; this was the familiar territory where the customs and religious traditions were well known. For the disciples, the people of Judea were "our kind of people." It was not too threatening to imagine taking the story of Jesus to the people of Judea.

The first circle would be the region of the Samaritans. The history between the Jews and the people of Samaria went back a long way, and frankly, there was some lingering bad blood between them. The Jews didn't much like the people of Samaria; called them "dogs" and other such unflattering names. To bring the story of Jesus to the Samaritans was going to take some work; the disciples were going to have to learn to think about these people in a new way. It was not going to be easy.

> ### Friend or Foe?
>
> Samaritans shared a common heritage with Jews (John 4:12), but were certainly not considered "kissing cousins." Tracing back their ancestry, the part of the family that moved into Samaria also adopted the religious practices of that region's inhabitants, and intermarried with them. The tension that existed in New Testament times may have been more about religion than race, but quite possibly the two reasons were blurred.

But most difficult of all was the call to take the good news about Jesus to the ends of the earth. All manner of strange and unusual people lived out there. They were foreigners. They didn't know anything about Jewish traditions and customs. To tell them the story of Jesus was going to require some real effort and commitment.

As the story of Acts unfolds, you see the disciples making forays into these unfamiliar places. And to their amazement they found people who were hungry to hear about Jesus and to join in with these "People of the Way," as the early Christians were called. Chapters 8, 9, and 10 of Acts tell about three pairs of people. Chapter 8 tells the remarkable story of Philip and the Ethiopian official. Chapter 9 tells about Saul and Ananias. And chapter 10 tells about the meeting between Peter and the Gentile soldier named Cornelius. In each of these pairs of people there is an "insider" and an "outsider."

Whenever we read a story in which there is an insider and an outsider, we have come to expect that the story will go in a particular way. The insider has it; the outsider doesn't; and the goal is for the insider to figure out how to persuade the outsider to get it. The early days of the American missionary movement were like that. We American Christians believed we had it, and out there was a world full of heathens who didn't have it—African tribespeople, Native Americans, Asians, people of Latin America, people who practiced different religions. We were the insiders, and they were the outsiders; we had it, and they did not.

That is the way we expect these stories in Acts to go. But in every case we are surprised. In the lesson for today, the insider is a man named Ananias; and the outsider is Saul, the persecutor of Christians.

Conversion

Many Bibles give this passage the title, "The Conversion of Saul." Let's talk about the word "conversion" for a minute. "Conversion" is one of those loaded church words. If you were going to write a short story about someone who was converted, you might write about some shiftless, ne'er-do-well bum, who is making an absolute mess of his life, then one day hears about Jesus and at once becomes a respectable, responsible citizen. He makes the radical move

> "One never becomes so wise or so adept at faith that conversion stops or one is immune from divine surprises."—William H. Willimon, *Acts*, Interpretation, 80.

from the wide, easy path that leads to destruction over to the straight and narrow. One minute he's here; the next minute he's there, a whole new person.

Now that makes for a good story, but I don't think that it tells the story of many of us. And it is not the way that the Bible wants us to understand conversion. In fact, conversion is not about picking up people and putting them in a whole new place. It is about someone's turning around to see things in a new way. The converted is the same person after the conversion as before; it's just that now that person is looking at things in a new way.

Furthermore, conversion is rarely a once-and-for-all-time event. For most Christians, conversion is an occurrence that happens many times over a lifetime. Take the apostle Peter as an example. How many conversions did Peter experience in his life? How many times did he find himself growing, gaining a new perspective on life?

"We progress by regression and go forward by falling backward. Such turning and helpless regression, accompanied by blindness, confusion, speechlessness, hunger, and childishness is, for this peculiar faith, the very beginning of wisdom."—William H. Willimon, *Acts*, Interpretation, 79.

Former president Jimmy Carter writes of his conversion experience in his book *Living Faith*. He tells that he was eleven years old when he accepted Jesus as his Savior and was born again. Then he goes on to say,

Being born again didn't happen to me when I was eleven. For me, it has been an evolutionary thing. Rather than a flash of light or a sudden vision of God speaking, it involved a series of steps that have brought me steadily closer to Christ. My conversion at eleven was just one of those steps. (Carter, 21–22)

Conversion as an ongoing experience of life is more like what happens to most people in the pew. The good news of the gospel has given us a new perspective with which to look at the world.

With that in mind, let's now turn to look at the conversion of Saul.

Stopped in His Tracks

Someone once described Saul as the number one agent for the FBI—the "Faith Bureau of Investigation." Saul was on a mission of defending the Jewish faith. This upstart group known as People of the Way was challenging the traditional Jewish way of looking at things, and Saul took it as his responsibility to keep the faith pure, to root out any false teaching. He was a man of strong faith, and that faith led him to seek out and eliminate anything that might threaten the historic beliefs of his ancestors.

Saul was willing to go to great lengths to put an end to this threat from the followers of Jesus. Stephen (see Acts 6 and 7) had already been executed for preaching about Jesus. Philip and Peter were still on the loose, and Saul was determined to stop them and the others. If "murderous threats" and violence were needed to accomplish the task, then so be it.

That is not to say that Saul was an evil person. On the contrary, Saul was a faithful, religious person. He was named after the first king of Israel; he was a member of the tribe of Benjamin. He grew up going to Sabbath school and learning well the traditions of Abraham, Isaac, and Jacob. Saul was the kind of person anyone would like to have as a member of the church: his faith was important to him, and he acted on his faith.

But then came that providential day that changed Saul's life forever. He was on his way to Damascus to round up any followers of Jesus who might be found there, when suddenly without any warning, a light from heaven flashed around him. Saul fell to his knees, and a voice from heaven spoke to him.

For many readers, this story of Paul's experience on the road to Damascus brings to mind another biblical conversion story—the call of Moses. Moses too met God through an unexpected light. Moses too heard the voice of God calling. Moses too wanted to know, "Who are you?" When Moses asked God's name, God answered, "I AM WHO I AM." (Ex. 3:13). And in that encounter with God, Moses was transformed from a murderer to a liberator, one called to set the people free. Might that same transformation be taking place in Saul's life?

Almost as if he is quoting Moses, when Saul hears the voice from heaven, he asks, "Who are you, Lord?" And the voice from heaven once again says, "I AM": "I am Jesus whom you are persecuting."

Blinded by the light and by the shocking revelation that the one he had been persecuting was the very One he sought to serve, for three days time stood still for Saul. For three days, he could think of nothing else. And when, after three days, his eyes were opened again, he found himself looking at the world in a whole new way. Before his conversion,

> "He who had intended to enter Damascus like an avenging fury was led by the hand, blind and helpless."—William Barclay, *Acts, Daily Study Bible*, 71.

Saul was a strong-willed, energetic, committed, zealous believer. After his conversion he was a strong-willed, energetic, committed, zealous believer . . . with a new way of looking at life. His conversion was a gift from God that enabled him to look at things in a new way.

The Conversion of Ananias

But Saul's is not the only conversion found here. Ananias was also converted. This is the real surprise of this story. We expect the outsider to be converted, but in all three of these chapters the insider is also converted, given a new way of looking at people and at the world. Look at how the story develops. The first part of the story tells about Saul's blinding experience. Then the spotlight turns on Ananias.

Ananias was a good man, a faithful believer, a disciple. He had a vision in which the Lord told him to look for a man named Saul. But Ananias said in so many words, "Are you sure you want me to do that? Don't you know about Saul? He's said and done a lot of terrible things to your followers. What good could possibly come from my talking to him?"

We can understand where Ananias was coming from. He had heard of Saul's reputation and couldn't believe that such a person could ever change. We are often like that too. There are people about whom we have already made up our minds. We know them; we know the way they think; we know the way they act; we don't particularly like them and would just as soon have nothing to do with them. Does this describe you in any way? Can you think of people that you have judged, labeled, and put in such a box?

Want to Know More?

About conversion and salvation?   See William H. Willimon, *Acts*, Interpretation (Atlanta: John Knox Press, 1988), 100–105, and William Barclay, *New Testament Words* (Philadelphia: Westminster Press, 1976), 268–76.

About the call of Moses? See James D. Newsome, *Exodus*, Interpretation Bible Studies (Louisville, Ky.: Geneva Press, 1998), 15–25.

Who can blame Ananias for not wanting to meet with Saul? For all he knew, Saul might be hiding a dagger under his robe. But the Lord told Ananias to go, and Ananias went. And when he met Saul, Ananias spoke one of the most daring statements of faith in the Bible. He said, "Brother Saul." Talk about a conversion! Ananias was converted in the way he looked at Saul. Ananias was given a new set of eyes and was able to see this former enemy in a new way. The enemy becomes a brother.

Who knows how Saul's conversion might have gone if Ananias had refused to do what the Lord asked him to do? All three of these stories that pair an insider and an outsider (Philip and the Ethiopian official, Ananias and Saul, Peter and Cornelius) demonstrate that conversion is an act of the whole community. Both the insider and the outsider are given a new set of eyes and a new way of looking at the world. The conversion is never fully complete until both parties turn around and look at things in a new way.

Back in the '70s, a little church in a small Mississippi town heard about the plight of the Vietnamese refugees who were looking to settle in the United States. They agreed to be a host congregation. They bought a small house, painted and cleaned it up, furnished it, put food in the pantry. And then the family came. At first the congregation was warm and accepting, but they quickly came to realize that these people were different. They spoke a funny language; they wore unusual clothes; they ate strange food; they were Buddhist. It was hard to cross over some of those barriers. Over time, fewer and fewer people stopped by to visit them. All except one dear lady whose name was Evelyn. Several times a week Evelyn would faithfully go by and visit this family. She did not have to do that. No one would have thought less of her if she too had quit visiting them. But there was just something different about Evelyn. She looked at this family through different eyes, and that enabled her to see them in a special way. Looking with the eyes of the kingdom, Evelyn could see that these people were no different from us; in fact, they were just like us—people hungry for love, people eager to hear some good news.

It wasn't just the Vietnamese who were converted to a new way of life. So was Evelyn, and both lives were richer for it.

A New Vision

The lessons from this story are many. It reminds us that our conversion is a gift from God, and that God is continually at work giving us a new, more faithful way of looking at the world. This story reminds us that God works in dramatic ways—in the voice that stops you in your tracks—and that God works in the whis-

> "True repentance spends less time looking at the past and saying, 'I'm sorry,' than to the future and saying, 'Wow.'"—Frederick Buechner, *Wishful Thinking: A Theological ABC* (New York: Harper & Row, 1973), 79.

pered nudges that open our eyes to a new vision of the people around us. The story reminds us that the call of every Christian is to bring good news and to celebrate that we are all brothers and sisters in Christ. And this story gives us the gift that enables us to look on the world with the eyes of the kingdom.

This story from Acts invites you to look at the people you meet through your kingdom eyes. They are people just like you—hungry for love and eager for good news. So share. Share scandalously without care of the cost. Share the love and good news of Christ with everyone you meet. You will see the world in a whole new way. And your life will be the richer for it.

? Questions for Reflection

1. This unit uses the image of concentric circles of relationships with people, moving from those we are close to in an inner circle to those we barely know at the outer circles. How many circles are there with you? How many people are in your inner circle? What does it take for someone to move from an inside circle out? What does it take for someone to move from an outside circle in?

2. How would you describe your conversion experience? What were some significant factors that influenced your conversion?

3. We meet an individual who coincidentally is named Ananias (see the previous unit.) Compare and contrast these two individuals. Compare the response of Ananias in verse 10 with that of Saul in verse 5. "Ananias" means something like "God is gracious." In this story, how does Ananias live up to his name? Knowing this name's meaning, does this help or hurt your understanding of the previous story? Why?

4. The previous question made much of the name of Ananias. However, it is the name of God or Jesus that is probably more prominent in this passage (verses 15–16). Using a concordance, check the references to the name of Jesus or God in Acts. What is the power and function of the name of Jesus (God) in the book of Acts?

5

Peter and Cornelius

The events of Acts 10 and 11 place the young Christian church at a crucial crossroads. How the church reacted to these events would determine whether or not the Christian church would be relegated to the position of a minor sect in a backwater corner of the world or would grow to be the significant influence all over the world which it is today. Had the church chosen to travel down the narrow, sectarian road, it may well have disappeared from world history. However, the church chose to take the daring and faithful step of opening its doors to all people. And that decision changed the course of the Christian church forever.

> "We usually do not realize how near Christianity was to becoming only another kind of Judaism."—William Barclay, *Acts*, Daily Study Bible, 86.

At the time, of course, there was nothing to indicate that this was such a monumental event. It seemed only like a meeting between two men—a Gentile soldier named Cornelius and the apostle Peter.

As you read this account of Peter and Cornelius, note how Luke, the masterful storyteller, keeps shining the spotlight back and forth from Cornelius to Peter and back again. Luke wants to keep us from focusing our attention on one or the other; he reminds us that both people are essential characters in this drama. This is not about Cornelius or about Peter; it's about the Holy Spirit's working in both their lives to accomplish something important. "The real 'hero' of the story, the 'star' of the drama is not Peter nor Cornelius but the gracious and prodding One who makes bold promises and keeps them, who finds a way even in the midst of human distinctions and partiality between persons" (Willimon, 99).

Cornelius, the Gentile Soldier

Luke gives some interesting details about Cornelius. We first learn that Cornelius had a connection to Rome. He was a Roman soldier, attached to the unit stationed in Caesarea. As a soldier, we can assume that Cornelius, like all soldiers, had sworn ultimate allegiance to Caesar. But we also see that Cornelius had a significant relationship to Judaism. He was a "devout man who feared God," and he demonstrated his piety through generous giving and prayer. He was knowledgeable about the practices of Judaism, and may even have participated in some of the activities of the synagogue. Presumably, he had reached a level of comfort required to balance his allegiance to Rome with his devotion to God. Little did he know that his comfortable world was about to be transformed.

> "Cornelius then was a man who was seeking after God, and as he sought God, God found him."—William Barclay, *Acts*, Daily Study Bible, 79.

About three o'clock one afternoon (this was one of the times of day when devout Jews would pray), Cornelius had a vision from heaven. Unaccustomed to such heavenly visitations, he was understandably terrified. He was told by the Spirit to contact a man in Joppa named Simon Peter. And immediately, Cornelius summoned his servants and sent them to Joppa.

Suddenly the spotlight shifts.

Simon Peter

The day after the visitation to Cornelius, the Holy Spirit spoke again—this time to Simon Peter. I am always glad when Peter makes an appearance in the biblical narrative. In contrast to so many of the Bible personalities who seem to get it right the first time, Peter's life of faith is characterized by fits and starts, steps forward and backward, acts of faith and acts of cowardice. Rather than one dramatic transformation, Peter's faith grows gradually with a number of course corrections along the way. Sometimes it looks like he's got it; then at other times it seems that he doesn't get it at all.

A helpful exercise for the class would be to research Peter's appearances in the Gospels and in Acts. William Barclay's little book *The Master's Men* has an interesting chapter about Peter. As Peter's story is told, we see him taking bold steps of faith and taking equally dramatic slides backward. Rather than one continuous smooth process of growing in faith, Peter's life of faith seems to lurch and swerve; it's a rocky ride.

It was about noontime when Peter went up on the roof of the house to pray. Without warning came this unusual vision. He saw a huge sheet being lowered down out of heaven containing all sorts of animals—both clean and unclean animals. The Jewish law was very clear about which animals fell into each category. As Peter looked, a voice from heaven spoke: "Peter, kill and eat." And Peter shot back, "No way. I will not eat anything that the law has declared unclean." But the voice spoke again, "Do not consider unclean what the Lord has declared clean." Three times this exchange took place.

It is hard for us to imagine the bind in which Peter found himself. Peter knew the laws of the Old Testament, and he tried his best to live by those laws. He also believed that to take even

> "It is not at all surprising that Peter should challenge this message three times. In fact, it is surprising that he challenged it *only* three times!"—Paul W. Walaskay, *Acts*, Westminster Bible Companion, 105.

the slightest liberty with those laws would have a terribly destructive effect. If people started to wink at this law or that law, before long the faith community would be destroyed.

> We must not read this story from the safe vantage point of a majority religion where broad-mindedness and toleration cost the majority nothing, but rather, read the story as it was first heard—from the minority point of view, people for whom a bit of pork or a pinch of incense [to Caesar] or a little intermarriage was a matter of life and death for the community. The dietary laws are not a matter of etiquette or peculiar culinary habits. They are a matter of survival and identity for Jews. (Willimon, 96)

Of course Peter was confused about the meaning of this heavenly vision. What could it all mean? While Peter was still pondering, he heard a knock on his door. Standing at his door were the men sent by the Gentile Cornelius. They came with an invitation for Peter to pay their master a visit. The fuzzy meaning of the dream began to become clearer to Peter. It dawned on Peter that this vision was not about animals; it was about people. The issue was not about clean and unclean animals; it was about people who were considered clean or unclean. Never before had the community of God even thought of God's love and promises being available or offered to unclean Gentiles. Now in dramatic form and with words that allow no room for quibbling—"What God has made clean, you must not call profane"—Peter is pushed to think about people, especially the Gentiles, in a whole new way.

And before Peter can even assimilate this new and radical message from God, he is asked to act on his new insight. No time to mull it over or cogitate. Armed with this powerful and graceful word, Peter is given the opportunity to act upon it.

Peter in the Home of Cornelius

Although Peter probably had no idea what might be waiting for him, he accepted the invitation and went to Caesarea. The next day Peter's trip to Caesarea would be a relatively short one geographically but it would be light years from anything he had ever thought or done before. Peter's willingness to visit the home of Cornelius was a violation of the Torah. Jewish law did not allow him to be the guest of a Gentile. Yet armed with a new insight into the faith, he headed there without hesitation. This next encounter with Cornelius and his household would be the first in a long line of Gentile witness opportunities still before him. Peter had to sense that something really big was going on here, for at risk in this visit was all he as a faithful believer had previously held sacred.

Cornelius had assembled a crowd to greet his guest. Warmly, humbly, Cornelius welcomed Peter to his home. And Cornelius gave a little speech, concluding, "So now all of us are here in the presence of God to listen to all that the Lord has commanded you to say" (v. 33). With that the spotlight turns back to Peter once again.

When Peter spoke, what he said bordered on blasphemy. "I understand that God shows no partiality." One of the central beliefs of Judaism had been the belief that they had an exclusive claim as God's chosen people. They had believed from the beginning, that God *does* show partiality—to the chosen people. Peter was now in very unfamiliar territory. As he was making his speech, we can almost see him rethinking the way he had understood Jesus. In this speech, Peter recited the life of Jesus beginning with his baptism, through his teachings and healings, to the crucifixion and resurrection. And as he recalled the life of Jesus, it became even clearer: Jesus is not Lord of some; *he is Lord of all.*

> "A vision of the Lordship of Christ, ruling with the Creator of heaven and earth, is the basis for Christian efforts at inclusiveness. One cannot have a Lord who is Lord of only part of creation."—William H. Willimon, *Acts,* Interpretation, 98.

While Peter was speaking, the Holy Spirit visited once again, this time being poured out upon the Gentiles gathered there. Some of the believers who had accompanied Peter were amazed to see this outpouring of the Spirit on Gentiles. Peter turned to his traveling companions and said, "What's to stop us from baptizing these people?" So these new believers were baptized and welcomed into the community.

The story is not over yet.

A Report to the Church in Jerusalem

Having had this radical vision and seen the outpouring of the Spirit in Caesarea, Peter had to report to the home office in Jerusalem about what had happened. Some people had heard about what Peter had done and were quick to criticize: "Why did you go to uncircumcised men and eat with them?"

Eating with Gentiles. Just as Jesus, during his lifetime, had been accused of eating with sinners, now Peter was being accused of eating with outsiders. Sharing a meal with another person has the effect of moving the relationship to a new level. It brings to mind the civil rights days of the '60s when African Americans, who were excluded from many restaurants, sought the right to eat in the same restaurants as whites. The student sit-in at the lunch counter in Greensboro, North Carolina, was intensified because it was an eating establishment.

In the early '70s I lived in a racially changing neighborhood. When the first black family moved to the house across the street, we welcomed them to the neighborhood, frequently visited in the front yard, were cordial and friendly. But several months passed before we invited them into our home for a meal. That act of sharing a meal together took the relationship to a new level. There is a greater intimacy and a higher level of acceptance between those who break bread together.

> "Placed here, and treated in this fashion, the scene serves as a warm, touching hint of the joyous new possibilities for community toward which God is leading both Jew and gentile."—William H. Willimon, *Acts*, Interpretation, 97.

There was another reason that there was objection to Peter's eating with the Gentiles. Eating a meal together was the central act of worship in the Christian church. The Eucharist, the fellowship meal, is the event in which every communicant stands equally before God. Around the Lord's Table there are no distinctions.

Robert McAfee Brown tells of a shipboard worship service in which he participated during World War II. The service was being conducted on the afterdeck near a gun turret. Thus, there was room for only three men at a time to come forward to receive Communion. The first three to come were the commanding officer of the ship, a fireman's apprentice and a black steward's mate. On the ship, there was a well defined and strictly observed class system, and each of these communicants came from a totally different stratum of the ship's hierarchy. But in the Communion service, all ranks were forgotten as the men knelt side by side before the table of their Lord (Brown, 155–56).

Want to Know More?

About the Roman military and officers? See Joel B. Green, Scot McKnight, and I. Howard Marshall, *Dictionary of Jesus and the Gospels* (Downers Grove, Ill.: InterVarsity Press, 1992), 548–49.

The influence of Peter in the early church? See Michael Goulder, *St. Paul versus St. Peter: A Tale of Two Missions* (Louisville, Ky.: Westminster John Knox Press, 1994)

About Jewish dietary laws? See Erhard S. Gerstenberger, *Leviticus: A Commentary*, Old Testament Library (Louisville, Ky.: Westminster John Knox Press, 1996), 128–46.

The divisions that separated Jew and Gentile went back many years. Was the church ready to take this dramatic inclusive step? No wonder Peter's critics objected to his eating with the Gentiles.

The church's reaction to Peter's bold new step sounds very contemporary. We can almost hear one of those first-century Christians whispering the seven last words of the church: "We've never done it that way before." Then, as now, there was a natural reluctance to do the new thing. The church hasn't changed all that much in 2,000 years!

Peter's report to the church in Jerusalem (11:4–17) recounted the events of the past several days—how the Holy Spirit had led him to Cornelius and how, when he was speaking to the people gathered at Cornelius's house, the Holy Spirit had descended upon them. He concludes by saying, "If then God gave them the same gift that he gave us when we believed in the Lord Jesus Christ, who was I that I could hinder God?" (v. 17). Peter's critics were silenced. Then the silence gave way to shouts of praise, as the people began to praise God for giving even to the Gentiles the repentance that leads to life.

The church's struggle with how to relate to the Gentiles was far from over. Differences of opinion continued. And yet the church had taken the daring first step that cracked open the doors of the church to welcome all people in.

The Lessons for Us

This story of Peter and Cornelius and the reaction of the church in Jerusalem gives some important lessons for Christians and the church today. One of the clearest lessons of this story is that God is in charge! At every step along the way, the Holy Spirit was directing things. The Holy Spirit led Cornelius to send for Peter; the Holy Spirit led Peter to accept Cornelius's invitation; the Holy Spirit filled those persons at the home of Cornelius. God is in charge—what good news! We have been given, as a free gift, the rule of God over our lives. No matter who we are, we all have the privilege of calling God in Christ, Lord. What is there about us which qualifies us for so high an honor? We have done nothing to earn or deserve this "status." Yet, not unlike Cornelius, we are included. "All" means "all"! We experience our inclusion among the people of God as evidence of the radical good news of the Gospel.

God reaches out to us with the free gift of acceptance and love. Our repentance, our life of faith, is our joyful response to this gift.

A second lesson from this story is that sometimes the Holy Spirit pushes us to think in a new way. Peter's heavenly vision forced him to a totally new way of looking at people. Is the Holy Spirit pushing us to think about people in new ways? Have we been guilty of allowing bias and prejudice to cloud our thinking? Could it be that the same Spirit who opened Peter's eyes to a clearer way of seeing is also doing the same in us?

> "Here is a God who takes me, 'Just as I am without one plea,' as we are fond of singing in the old hymn, but encounters with this God do not leave us just as we are."—William H. Willimon, *Acts*, Interpretation, 104.

This leads us to a third, and equally important, lesson from this story—how we are to relate to one another. The church of the first century had a clear understanding of insiders and outsiders, who was included and who was to be excluded . . . until this Spirit-directed meeting between Peter and Cornelius blew those notions away. Through the centuries that followed, the church has continued to wrestle with the issue of inclusiveness. It is still true today. Barriers remain. Opening the doors of the church continues to be an issue today. Who are the Gentiles of today? Who are the ones excluded from the church? Maybe it is the homosexual, the person with AIDS, or the poor. The fact is that they frequently feel excluded from the church. The eleven o'clock hour on Sunday morning remains the most racially segregated hour of the week. Is that because of personal preference and individual choice, or is it the result of subtle (or perhaps not-so-subtle) hints that some people are not welcome? Remember, Jesus is Lord, not of some, but of all.

Who are the Corneliuses in your community? Are there people who feel like outsiders? The church today needs to be continually examining the ways that it may be excluding people. Certainly the church may be a more comfortable place if everyone is "just like us," but the Spirit does not call us to be comfortable. The Spirit calls us to be faithful. If we are to be the kind of community that the Holy Spirit calls us to be, then we need to be willing to welcome all God's people. An African American friend said, "Too many people think that integration means 'you become like us.' But real integration means that both of us change into something brand new."

> **Things will never be the same**
>
> "The story of Cornelius, which ends with Peter's speech to the assembly at Jerusalem, is the longest narrative in Acts, a seven-act drama of sixty-six verses. Judged solely on the basis of the amount of space Luke gives to the story, we know that we are dealing with a crucial concern of Acts, a pivot for the entire book, a turning point in the long drama of redemption."—William H. Willimon, *Acts*, Interpretation, 95.

This encounter between Peter and Cornelius blew the church wide open. Imagine what the church today would look like if, back in the first century, the branch that wanted to keep the Gentiles out had prevailed. The church would probably have died out, a relic of ancient history. Because those early Christians took the bold step to open the doors of the church, you and I have been allowed in. Thanks be to God.

? Questions for Reflection

1. This unit suggests that the openness of Peter to Cornelius may have taken the church toward a more prominent role in its history—one choice with far-reaching consequences. Think back in your own life. What are some of the choices you have made with far-reaching consequences (perhaps in selecting a vocation, attending school, a relationship, etc.)? What were the factors that influenced your choices?

2. Cornelius is described in this unit as one who could "balance his allegiance to Rome with his devotion to God" (cf. Luke 20:25). What helps someone balance the differing pressures of life? How

does one give allegiance to family, to work, or to the state, and keep one's devotion to God as well?

3. Cornelius and Peter both have visions filled with elaborate details. Each go on to tell of those experiences. They are both witnesses (Acts 1:8) to what they have experienced. What are the experiences of your faith of which you could witness?

4. There is a sense of providence in this passage—that the characters cannot or should not stand in the way of God (10:47 and 11:17). What are other examples of the providence of God from your reading of Acts so far?

6 Acts 15

The Jerusalem Council

My father was a Presbyterian minister who grew up in a time when the "rules" for Christian living were stricter than they are now. In my father's rigid upbringing, movies and other such frivolous entertainment were regarded as morally questionable, so he never went to movies. After graduating from seminary, he accepted a call to a struggling new congregation. To help the church grow, he made a concerted effort to reach out to the young people and to draw them into the church. One Saturday he organized a youth gathering at the church. It was well attended and a good start to what he hoped would grow. When the program ended, some of the young people decided to go to a movie, and they invited my father to go along. What was he to do? Should he refuse to go, citing his principles? Or should he go along in order to help build a relationship with the youth? It was for him a genuine moral dilemma.

The decision my father faced was a micro-version of a crucial issue that was before the early church. It was an issue that would have far-reaching consequences for the Christian church, and the decision did not come easily. In struggling with the issue, the church experienced "no small dissention and debate" (v. 2).

The Nature of the Problem

Jesus' last words to the disciples before his ascension into heaven were a charge to them to "be my witnesses in Jerusalem, in all Judea and Samaria, and to the ends of the earth" (Acts 1:8). Empowered by the Holy Spirit, the followers of Jesus did just that. While Jerusalem remained the "home office," disciples of Jesus fanned out across the eastern end of the Mediterranean with the gospel story. Peripatetic Paul was the most energetic in his missionary efforts. His first missionary journey, which is recorded in Acts 13–14, lasted about three years and took him and Barnabas (see chapter 3 of this study) to such exotic places as Seleucia, Cyprus, and two Antiochs! Everywhere they went they found people who were receptive to the proclamation of God's love in Christ. (They also encountered people who were less than receptive—as in Lystra, for example, where Paul was stoned and left for dead!).

Jerusalem functioned as a headquarters for the early church.

Since every one of the first followers of Jesus (and Jesus himself) traced their religious roots back to the Old Testament, to King David, to Moses, to Abraham, it was natural that they would be drawn toward those who shared this heritage as they told the story of Jesus. For example, whenever Paul would enter a new town to tell the story of Jesus, he would first go to the familiar surroundings of the synagogue. Many of the first Christians came directly from this rich tradition. They continued to observe the Old Testament laws that governed the kind of foods to eat and many other aspects of daily living. The customs of Judaism were very dear to these Jewish Christians.

However, at the same time, there were also people who had not been raised in the traditions of Judaism who were being drawn to the gospel message that the disciples were preaching. These Gentile converts to Christianity were evidence that the disciples were taking seriously Jesus' call to be witnesses "to Samaria and to the ends of the earth." Acts 8 tells us that Philip (v. 5) and Peter and John (v. 25) all proclaimed the good news in the towns and villages of Samaria. The doors of the church were cracking open a little wider to these people who had not been welcome before. The Christian church was changing as people from different traditions and cultures were finding their way into the church, and it was inevitable that the different cultures would clash.

The presence of both Jewish Christians and Gentile Christians was a source of growing tension in the church. The Jewish Christians did not oppose preaching the gospel to Gentiles, but they felt strongly that the only way these Gentile adherents could be included in the covenant family was by adopting the practices of Judaism—particularly circumcision. From the time of Abraham, circumcision had been the sign of the covenant and its blessings, and the Jewish Christians felt that it was an essential prerequisite for participation in the Christian community.

By contrast, those Gentile Christians did not see any reason that they should have to become Jews in order to become Christian. They saw no connection between the physical ritual of circumcision and their acceptance of Jesus as Lord.

The tensions between Jewish Christians and Gentile Christians grew to the point that something had to be done. From the hinterlands, word filtered back to the apostles in Jerusalem about the success that Paul and others were having among the Gentiles. The apostles decided to call a council in Jerusalem to discuss this important issue.

Corroborating Witness?

Paul refers to the meeting in Jerusalem in Galatians 2:1–10, though Paul's "take" on the incident is slightly different than Luke's account in Acts. In Paul's version, *he* convinces Peter of the hypocrisy of Peter's ways about demanding circumcision. In Acts, Peter agrees with Paul at the meeting because of Peter's own experience with Cornelius. For some suggestions at reconciling these different versions, see Paul Walaskay, *Acts*, Westminster Bible Companion, 150–51.

The Jerusalem Council

The church in Jerusalem was the center of power of the early Christian church. The apostles remained in Jerusalem, so it made sense that whenever questions arose concerning faith or doctrine, ritual or practice, the apostles in Jerusalem would settle those questions. To decide the conflict that was brewing between the Jewish Christians and the Gentile Christians, a council was called in Jerusalem. All leaders of the young Christian church were there—Peter, James, John, and the other apostles. And the issue before them was this: what would be the rules to govern life together in the Christian church? Should a person be required to observe the laws of Judaism in order to be a Christian? Or could one be a Christian and not keep all those laws? What were the essentials for life together?

At the Jerusalem Council, there were people on both sides of the issue, and the Bible says that there was considerable dissension and debate. Anyone who has ever attended a church convention can easily visualize what the Jerusalem Council must have looked like. As at any church meeting, there were probably motions and amendments. There were calls for "points of order." Listen closely and you might still be able to hear the moderator recognizing the speaker at microphone three, and rapping the gavel to call the group to order. Throughout the debate there were reasoned and well-thought-out speeches, and probably also some emotional ranting and raving . . . not unlike church meetings of today.

> "These church meetings with people crowding the microphone, bickering over budgets, basing their vote on their personal prejudices rather than on the Word of God—how many Christians have had the fire of their initial enthusiasm extinguished by unpleasant church meetings?"—William H. Willimon, *Acts*, Interpretation, 128.

Today we might ask similar questions. Are there beliefs or practices that are considered essential in a covenant community? Is a person expected to hold a certain position on the doctrine of election, or the meaning of baptism, or tithing, or going to the movies? Is a person's race or economic status a factor for church membership?

When persons join the Presbyterian Church (U.S.A.), they "declare their intention to participate actively and responsibly in the worship and mission of the church" (*Book of Order*, W-4.2003). Working for the common good of the church and its members—should that be considered necessary for admission into the church?

Dietrich Bonhoeffer, in his little book *Life Together*, said that life in the Christian community should include worship, scripture reading, hymn singing, prayer, and table fellowship (Bonhoeffer, 40–67). Are these practices imperative for those who wish to be a part of the community of faith? Or should there be any requirements for membership at all?

> "Rather than do what churches often do on such occasions—flee from the fight, submerge our differences, or else storm off in a huff—the apostles demonstrate that the gospel has given them the resources to confront controversy without being destroyed by it."—William H. Willimon, *Acts*, Interpretation, 131–32.

Emotions ran high at Jerusalem because it was a vitally important issue. It was a question of essentials—what should be the ground rules for living together in the Christian community? They discussed; they argued; they prayed. And finally they came up with their answer.

Life Together

In the first century, when the council at Jerusalem pondered this question, they came up with the following list of essentials. James was the apostle who presented the report (vv. 19–21). James says, in effect, "I have determined that the following things are necessary for our life together: don't eat meat offered to idols, keep from fornication, and eat no blood nor any animal that has been strangled. That's it; just those essentials."

That's it? They concluded nothing about circumcision or Sabbath observance? What an odd list of rules! Don't they sound a little trifling, a little irrelevant, just plain out of touch? Nevertheless, this is the list that the early church leaders decided upon: eat no meat contaminated by idolatry, keep from fornication, and eat no meat that has been strangled or has blood.

> With a long history of legal tradition that could have been imposed, "James decided for God rather than for precedent."—Luke T. Johnson, *Decision Making in the Church* (Philadelphia: Fortress Press, 1983), 84.

I want to suggest two different ways of looking at this unusual list of rules and regulations. One way we can look at this list is that it is not all that is expected of someone, but it is a place to start. For these new Christians coming into the community of faith these rules established a starting place for their life together. And building upon this starting place, the community grows.

Perhaps a couple of examples will help to clarify this point. A woman went to her pastor to talk about prayer. She said, "I've been doing just what you told us to do; I've been praying 30 minutes every day, but I'm just not getting anywhere. I pray for this and I pray for that, but never seem to get any answers to my prayers." So the minister said, "Okay, what I would like for you to do is to take the first five minutes of your prayer time and use it to say Thanks to God. Just five minutes, then you can use the rest of the time to ask for the things you want." A couple of weeks later, the woman came back to the minister and told him that things had changed. She quickly discovered that five minutes was not enough time to say Thanks to God, and before long she

> "The paradox of Christianity is that the way to victory is through surrender; and the way to power is through admitting one's own helplessness."—William Barclay, *Acts,* Daily Study Bible, 115.

was using 25 minutes for saying Thank You and only 5 minutes for asking." You see what happened? Is five minutes all that is required for expressing our thanks to God? No, but it's a start. And if we start there, we discover our life of prayer maturing and growing.

A recent television interview provides another example. A Christian layman, who is extremely generous in his giving, told how his giving practices developed. He was very financially successful in his business, but had never acquired a taste for giving; he would give a few dollars here and there, but that was all. One day his pastor came to him and said, "It's well known that you are making a lot of money, but that you are not giving well. I want you to do something with me. Name an amount of money that you could give away and not really miss it—$5,000? $10,000?" The man answered, "Well, I could give away $5,000 with no problem." So the minister told him to clear his calendar for the day; they went to the bank, cashed a check for $5,000 and off they went. They went to the neighborhood soup kitchen, where the man saw the good work that was being done there, and he made a donation. They went to where a group of volunteers were working on a house for Habitat for Humanity, and the man was moved by what he saw, and he made a donation. They went to a day-care center for the elderly, to the shelter for battered women, to the pharmacy for the indigent, and every place they went, he saw the good work that was being done, and he made a donation. That day of seeing for himself first-hand the kind of self-giving service that people are willing to do for others, and getting a taste of the good feeling that comes from supporting those programs changed that man. From that day on, he was hooked on giving. That day he experienced the joy of giving, and he wanted to do more. The $5,000 that he gave that day was not all that was required of him, but it was a starting point, and from there his life of stewardship and giving grew.

Maybe it works the same with this list of rules in Acts. This odd collection of "do's and don'ts" form a starting point for one's growth in living the Christian life.

There is also a second way of looking at this list of rules. As one reads this list of prohibitions—things *not* to do—it seems that each one could also be said in a positive form—something *to* do. Take the prohibition against fornication, for example. It was true then and is still true today that unrestrained sexual activity undermines family life and society as a whole. Promiscuity, sexual immorality, will kill a family and eventually a society.

Therefore this same rule could be written to do whatever is necessary to build up family, to build community, to promote the highest good for all.

Or what about the rule that forbids contact with idolatry? Idolatry diminishes the worship of the one true God, and that, in turn, destroys the human spirit, the soul. So this prohibition against idolatry could be written positively to read that we are to do everything in our power to build up the spirit, which will put us in touch with God our Creator. That, of course, is the reason to encourage people in regular worship attendance. Will worship attendance make the problems of life go away? No, of course not. But regular worship will remind us of God's power which is greater than our own, and in that power we will find peace and our troubled spirits will be calmed.

Or finally, what about those rules about the kind of meat to eat? In the early days of the Old Testament when these rules were first formulated, they did not know what we know about how to preserve and cook meat properly. But they did know that if it was done improperly, it could kill a person. So this prohibition against eating certain kinds of meat is to help save lives. Here again, this could be stated positively. It could read to do everything in our power to save life rather than diminish or destroy life.

Want to Know More?

About the life of Paul and his journeys? See C. K. Barrett, *Paul: An Introduction to His Thought* (Louisville, Ky.: Westminster John Knox Press, 1994), 1–21.

About circumcision? See Gerald F. Hawthorne, Ralph P. Martin, and Daniel G. Reid, *Dictionary of Paul and His Letters* (Downers Grove, Ill.: InterVarsity Press, 1993), 137–39.

About growing in the Christian Faith? See Craig Dykstra, *Growing in the Life of Faith: Education and Christian Practices* (Louisville, Ky.: Geneva Press, 1999). For practices and disciplines, see John Westerhoff, *Spiritual Life: The Foundation for Preaching and Teaching* (Louisville, Ky.: Westminster John Knox Press, 1994), and Marjorie J. Thompson, *Soul Feast: An Invitation to the Christian Spiritual Life* (Louisville, Ky.: Westminster John Knox Press, 1995). For a collection of daily devotional readings, see William Barclay, *Growing in Christian Faith: A Book of Daily Readings* (Louisville, Ky.: Westminster John Knox Press, 2000).

As the young Christian church sought to establish their rules for life together, they realized that there were some things that were essential: protect human life, protect the human spirit and a relationship to God, protect the community so that all can live and work in harmony and peace. And these things are just as important today as they were centuries ago.

Now back to the decision my father had to make—which would you do? Would you hold on to the traditions you learned as a child or would you join the young people and go to the movies?

? Questions for Reflection

1. In the middle of this unit, the question is asked, "Are there beliefs or practices that are considered essential in a covenant community?" Are there? If so, what are they and why are they essential? If not, why not?
2. Peter, Paul, and James are leaders in this passage. Up to this point, Peter has been the prominent character. It is James who makes the big decision and then from this time on, Paul moves into the limelight. How are leaders chosen in churches today? How are decisions handled in matters affecting churches today?
3. The Jerusalem Council decided to write a letter to the Gentiles. Was the letter to accept them, or to clarify what the Gentiles must do to be accepted, or did the letter serve another purpose? How so? How would you respond to a letter from the denominational headquarters?
4. Peter makes several comments in verses 7–11. Among them are that God "has made no distinction between [the Gentiles] and us" and that "we will be saved through the grace of the Lord Jesus, just as they will." Using a concordance, find other verses in the New Testament that support Peter's claims.

7 Acts 17:16–34

Paul in Athens

Telling the story of Jesus is not a "one size fits all" enterprise. Different situations require different methods of proclamation. A preacher addressing a congregation that has gathered on a Sunday morning to listen politely to the sermon can take a deliberate approach. In that setting the sermon can develop in a carefully constructed way with points and poems and pithy illustrations. ("I heard a story about . . . ")

But what if the audience is disinterested or even hostile? How does the preacher approach the task? The street corner preacher trying to engage the hurried passersby as they wait to cross the street does not have the luxury of carefully developing an idea. Of necessity, such a sermon must quickly engage the listener. It will have a much different preaching style from the typical Sunday sermon.

There is a common thread in all styles, however. The best preaching and the most effective way of telling the story of Jesus requires that the preacher engage the listener on his or her own ground. A good preacher is clear about the subject and also aware of the needs and interests of the listeners. Perhaps that was what made Paul such a powerful evangelist. He was certainly clear about his message, and he also worked to understand his audience. Nowhere was that more evident than in the passage that is today's lesson.

On the Road Again

With the experiences of his first missionary journey still fresh in his mind, it was not long before Paul was ready to leave Jerusalem and to set out again. On the second journey, accompanied part of the time by Silas, Paul went even farther. It has been estimated that Paul covered some ten thousand miles in his missionary travels—no mean feat considering the often-poor conditions of the roads and methods of transportation available in the first century. Paul had a story to tell, and he was not going to be stopped. On this journey his travels took him into Greece, and eventually to Athens.

In the City of Socrates

Athens was the heart of Greek culture and philosophy. The golden age of Athens had been some five hundred years earlier during the time of the great philosophers, Socrates and Plato. By the time Paul arrived, Athens was well past its prime. Nevertheless, Athens was still considered the greatest university city of its time, and intellectuals from all over were drawn to it. One of the favorite activities of the Athenian intelligentsia was to gather in the marketplace to argue and debate any new thing that came along. (If you use your imagination, you can almost see them sitting at the sidewalk café, sipping a cup of cappuccino, and discussing the most important issues of the day.)

> "Their legendary Athenian curiosity leads Paul into the Areopagus, where the Athenians spent their days doing what intellectuals enjoy—relieving their boredom by searching for new ideas. Novelty attracts their attention more quickly than truth."—William H. Willimon, *Acts*, Interpretation, 142.

Paul spent time in the marketplace, listening in on their conversations. He heard them defending their various philosophies. Some of them espoused a philosophy called Epicureanism. The Epicureans didn't really hold much belief in any god; they believed that the gods were remote from the world and didn't particularly care about what was going on in it. The "proof" for their position was the suffering that was all around. They reasoned that if the gods cared, there would not be such suffering. Therefore they concluded that we might as well live it up and get whatever pleasure we can out of life.

> "Their religious yearning, even though a bit of a scandal to a monotheistic Jew, is the inarticulate and uninformed yearning of the pagan for the God whom only the Scriptures can disclose."—William H. Willimon, *Acts*, Interpretation, 143.

Others there held to a philosophy known as Stoicism. The Stoics believed that all life came from the mind of Zeus, and therefore we are out of control and we may as well play the hand we are dealt because there's nothing we can do about it.

The two different philosophies made for some interesting and heated discussions. Those were the people to whom Paul was taking the story of Jesus. Paul was eager to tell them about Jesus, but how? In his travels Paul had preached to all types of people—rich and poor, slave and free. He had seen that people of all strata of society were hungry to hear the good news. But would that be true of these intellectuals of Athens? How could Paul reach them?

Paul and the Philosophers

Paul had done his homework. He had studied their various philosophies; he knew about all their gods. He could enter into their culture. And he did. As he talked, he used words they were very familiar with. Quoting Greek poets and philosophers, Paul hooked them in. "The God who made the world and everything in it . . ." (v. 24)— that is language straight out of Greek Stoic philosophy. And later Paul says, "In him we live and move and have our being" (v. 28); that is a quotation from a Greek philosopher named Epimenides. And "For we too are his offspring" (v. 28) is a line from a well-known Greek poet, Aratus.

Do you see what Paul was doing? He was engaging the people of Athens by using their own language and philosophies to establish a common ground with them. He was using language that they were familiar with to make his point. In short, Paul came to them, on their terms, speaking a language they understood. Paul began by entering into their culture, their way of thinking.

When Paul came to Athens, he saw quickly that there were people there who needed to hear the story of Jesus, who needed to hear a word of good news. But in order to give them a chance to hear it, he first had to connect with them, to establish a common ground so that they would continue to listen. So he went to them. What Paul might have done when he arrived in Athens was to set up office hours, hang out a shingle, and advertise that anyone who wanted to learn about Jesus could make an appointment between the hours of 9 and 4 Monday through Thursday. He could have waited for them to come to him, but instead he went to them.

"The church, rather than standing back from pagan religiosity, pointing our fingers in righteous indignation, should, like Paul in Athens, minister to their searching."— William H. Willimon, *Acts*, Interpretation, 143.

Paul reached out to the people of Athens with the same kind of grace with which God reached out to the world. God might have waited for us to make the first move, but instead God came to us in the person of Jesus. God brought the message of love and salvation to us in a form with which we could identify and used language that we could understand. God came to us.

Following Paul's Model

One thing that this story about Paul in Athens does for us is to give us a model to follow as we undertake the task of telling others the good news of Jesus. It reminds us that if we are going to connect with other people, we need to take the initiative, to reach out to them.

Sometimes those connections are easily made. Every day, the followers of Jesus are rubbing shoulders with people who are hungry to hear a word of good news. As they live their faith in their daily lives—in the workplace, in the schools, in offices and factories, on the golf course—they already have some common ground with the people they are meeting every day. Those who are in the business world, for example, know well the language of commerce and industry; they have an established connection with the people whose paths they cross. They already know some of the stresses and joys that their colleagues are going through. They don't have to cross a huge gulf to enter into their environment and culture. It's the same in other fields as well. Teachers have a common ground with other teachers; assembly line workers have a common ground with their coworkers; parents have a common ground with other parents. In many cases, the connections are easily made as we reach out to others. We don't always have to go to the same lengths as Paul in order to tell the good news.

Other times, however, the connections are not so easily made. As our society becomes more mobile and more diverse, we become less homogeneous than in earlier days. This

Want to Know More?

About Epicureanism or Stoicism? See Wayne A. Meeks, *The Moral World of the First Christians*, Library of Early Christianity (Philadelphia: Westminster Press, 1986), 40–64, and Calvin J. Roetzel, *The Letters of Paul: Conversations in Context*, 4th ed. (Louisville, Ky.: Westminster John Knox Press, 1998), 19–36.

About the Greco-Roman pantheon? See Robert M. Grant, *Gods and the One God*, Library of Early Christianity (Philadelphia: Westminster Press, 1986), 19–71.

About resurrection? See Shirley C. Guthrie, *Christian Doctrine*, rev. ed. (Louisville, Ky.: Westminster John Knox Press, 1994), 270–87.

is especially true in the big cities, but even in the small towns, the complexion of the community is changing. Frequently in our daily round of activities, we encounter people whom we do not know and with whom we do not have an automatic connection. As followers of Jesus, we are called to reach out to them as well. How can we take the good news of the gospel to these people?

In either case, the burden rests on us. We are the ones with good news to share; it's our task to find the way to share it. Such was Paul's experience in Athens: he knew that he could not expect the people to come to him, so he reached out to them.

The Unknown God

Athens was not only known for the intellectuals who were drawn there. Athens was also a very religious city—at least it seemed so. It was said that there were more statues of the gods in Athens than in all the rest of Greece put together, and that in Athens it was easier to meet a god than a person (Barclay, 130). As Paul moved throughout the city, everywhere he turned were these idols (v. 16)—marble, gold, bronze, of all shapes and sizes. Greek mythology had a god for every occasion. There was Ares, the god of war, and Aphrodite, the goddess of love. There was Poseidon, god of the sea, and Hestia, goddess of

Athens was filled with temples to gods, known and unknown.

the hearth. There was a god in charge of wisdom, another who made the crops grow. Practically every aspect of human life was under the purview of some god or goddess. Temples and statues of the various gods and goddesses were found throughout the city of Athens. Surely Paul, although distressed by their pantheon of gods, was impressed with the religious atmosphere of Athens. "I see how extremely religious you are in every way," Paul said to the Athenians.

One of the statues bore this inscription: "To an unknown God." Try to imagine how such a shrine might have come into being. When the Greek soldiers went off to war, they knew they needed the gods on their side, so they prayed to the god of war. When they planted their crops they knew they needed the gods on their side, so they prayed to the god of the harvest. But they also knew that all their attempts to categorize a god for every occasion were inadequate. No matter how much they might invent a god to cover every situation and condition, they understood that the divine presence was greater than that. This "unknown god" was the God who could not be categorized, could not be limited, could not be contained.

At some time or another every believer has encountered God in a surprising and unexpected way. People often relate that in the midst of a crisis when all seemed out of control, they experienced a peace and calm that they could not explain. They could only attribute it to the unexpected presence of God. Sometimes we encounter the surprising God in the ordinary events of life—in the times that we are aware that life is good beyond our own doing. Like the people of Athens, we too know that God is too vast to be contained and that the surprising, limitless God comes to us in all times and places.

Paul said to the people of Athens: "Your unknown God, the God who cannot be contained or limited—that's the God I want to tell you about" (v. 23).

Paul's Sermon

In proclaiming to the Athenians "the unknown God," Paul used his best evangelistic skills. Yes, Paul employed language and philosophical ideas that the Athenians understood in order to establish common ground and capture their attention. But he well knew that there would come a point when he would move beyond their accepted ideas to proclaim the radical truth of the gospel. Let's look now at Paul's sermon (vv. 22–31).

> "It is no unknown God but a Risen Christ with whom we have to deal."—William Barclay, *Acts*, Daily Study Bible, 132.

As the sermon begins, you can almost hear Paul singing "This Is My Father's World" (v. 24). Paul celebrates God the creator. For many people, an observation of the natural world—the mysterious beauty of the countless sparkles of light in the night sky, the delicate intricacy of a rose, "rocks and trees, skies and seas"—leads them to conclude that there must be a God. A world so complex and so beautiful could not be an accident. The Greeks of Paul's day understood that truth, just as people do today.

However, looking at the natural world can take a person only so far in understanding about God. "Too many people look at growing grass and see only cells dividing, or into the sky and see masses of matter and swirling gas. Natural theology is hardly more than preliminary instruction. Something else is needed" (Willimon, 143–44).

"[B]ut now in Christ the full blaze of the knowledge of God has come and the day of excuses is past."—William Barclay, *Acts, Daily Study Bible*, 132.

Fortunately for us, God did not leave us to grope around in the dark. God revealed God's self to us in the person of Jesus (v. 31). In the life, death, and resurrection of Jesus, our understanding of God is taken to a whole new level. Belief in the resurrection of Jesus cannot come through observation of the natural world. In the natural world death appears to have the final word. To affirm the resurrection of Jesus moves one beyond logical observation to a level where only faith can go, a faith that supersedes logic. Without any physical evidence, only by leaping to this other level can we trust in God's power to bring life out of death. A belief in the power of God to raise Jesus from the dead is at the very heart of the gospel. It is this leap of faith that allows us to lift our eyes above the natural world to see a kingdom world in which the Lord God Omnipotent reigns.

Sadly, it was a leap that some people were (and are) unwilling to make.

The Reaction to Paul's Sermon

There were three distinct reactions to Paul's sermon. (1) Some scoffed. Then, as now, some people found Christianity hopelessly out of touch, a curiosity, but nothing of real value. (2) Some wanted to hear more, but were unwilling to make a commitment. How easy it is to put off until tomorrow the decision to serve Christ! (3) Some believed. Did they have all their questions answered? Probably not. But they believed that the God revealed in the life, death, and resurrection of Christ was worth the risk of faith.

Some Challenges

The story of Paul's encounter with the philosophers in Athens challenges us in several ways. First, it challenges us to think about our calling to tell the story of Jesus to others. It reminds us of the need to be sensitive to the needs and circumstances of others so that we can connect with them on a meaningful level. Second, this story also challenges us to open our eyes to the unexpected ways that we have experienced God's presence in our lives. Just as the people of Athens acknowledged "an unknown God" who could not be boxed in or limited, so we

> Therein is the risk. We profess that we will "follow Christ," hoping all the while that the path leads not where we would not go. Therein is the reward—that indeed it does.

too are to be receptive to the surprising movement of God among us. Finally, this story challenges us to take the leap of faith to trust in God's power, to acknowledge God's sovereignty, and to see the world through eyes of the kingdom.

? Questions for Reflection

1. This unit introduces several of the philosophies that were popular in the time of Paul, each with its own perspective to offer about the sovereignty of God and the problem of evil. What are some of the philosophies that are popular today that deal with life, death, the afterlife, evil, etc.? How do these philosophies differ from Christian perspectives on the same issues?
2. Evangelism and missions can be points of tension for Christians. Though many might be supportive of telling others about Christ, they are uneasy doing the telling themselves. Why do you suppose this is? What are some ways of connecting with others to tell them the gospel?
3. Verses 30–34 suggest that in this case, it is the resurrection that becomes the hinge-pin for acceptance of the gospel. What do you believe about the resurrection? Drawing on the discussion from previous units, is belief in the resurrection one of the essentials of the faith? Why or why not?
4. Paul used the phrase "to an unknown God" (vv. 23–24) to call attention to the Lord, maker of heaven and earth. What are some ways that God is known to us? In an ironic sense, there are also aspects of God that are puzzling and unknown. What are some things that make God seem unknown to us?

8 Acts 16:11-15; 18:1-4, 18-28

Women in the New Testament Church

In first-century Palestine, differences that distinguished and divided people were a fact of life. There were socioeconomic differences that placed people in classes ranging from persons with wealth and privilege to slaves who had no rights of their own. In the Roman world, "there was virtually no movement out of the social class to which one was born nor any expectation of movement. Classes were hereditary, fixed at birth" (Willimon, 138). There were also racial and ethnic differences. Jews placed great value on their racial purity, and their laws limited intermingling with non-Jews. The Jews believed that they were God's chosen people, and Gentiles were a cut below. In addition, there were gender differences that placed men and women in unequal standing. These various socioeconomic, racial, and gender barriers were widely accepted as simply among life's givens.

One of the places that these differences could be seen was in the architecture of the Temple in Jerusalem. The Temple was a large area made up of a series of courtyards. The outermost courtyard was called the Court of the Gentiles; anyone was allowed to come into it. Next was the Court of the Women,

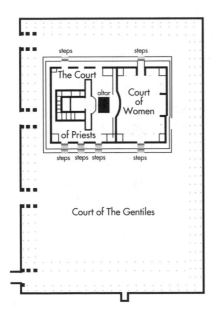

The courts of the Temple.

64

into which any Israelite—man or woman—could come. Next was the Court of the Israelites; only Hebrew men were allowed inside. Finally, surrounded by the Court of the Israelites, which included a gallery on three sides, there was the Court of the Priests—priests only allowed. The design of the Temple courtyards assumed a hierarchy that placed Hebrews above Gentiles and Hebrew men above Hebrew women.

It was definitely a man's world. Male power and authority dominated politics, religion, and even family life. The laws and customs made sure that women were regarded as subordinate to men. Women in that day had one primary responsibility: to marry and produce an heir. In the Jewish religion, women were definitely second-class citizens. One example is that for Jewish worship, ten adult males were required to have a congregation. If there were 100 women but only 9 men, there was not a duly constituted congregation. Also there was a traditional saying that advised men: "Talk not much with a woman. . . . Everyone that talks much with a woman causes evil to himself, and desists from the words of Torah, and his end is he inherits Gehinnom [Hell]" (*Pirke Aboth* 1:5; cited in Walaskay, 157)

That was the world into which the Christian church was born.

Unity in a Divided World

One of the most significant contributions of the Christian church was its willingness to examine the accepted cultural mores and to challenge them. It was the belief that in Christ all things are made new. Paul's radical affirmation in Galatians says it boldly: "There is no longer Jew or Greek; there is no longer slave or free; there is no longer male and female; for all of you are one in Christ Jesus" (Gal. 3:28).

We have seen in other places in Acts how the church struggled to come to a new understanding of the relationship between Jewish Christians and Gentile Christians. The change was slow and did not come without conflict, but gradually the church began to accept Gentiles as full participants in the Christian community.

> **For richer and poorer**
>
> In chapter 16 of Acts, "rich business people are touched by the gospel [vs. 14] as well as slave girls (vss. 16–18) and middle class jailers (vss. 30–34)."—Charles H. Talbert, *Acts*, Knox Preaching Guides (Atlanta: John Knox Press, 1984), 69.

The texts we are studying in this unit show that the church also came to a new understanding of the role of women in the church.

Even though the cultural backdrop against which the church was set saw women as inferior to men, women played a vitally important role in the church. As William Willimon points out, "When compared to conventional Jewish and Greco-Roman ideas about women, the church must have seemed radical in the way it welcomed women and featured them as leaders and prophets" (Willimon, 137).

It must be admitted, however, that change in the understanding about women did not come overnight. In many places the New Testament seems to accept the culture's view of women. Sometimes the Bible appears to present women as second-class people. In Acts 1, for example, there is a list of those who were present for one of Jesus' resurrection appearances. Many of the men are listed by name—Peter, John, James, Andrew, and others—"together with certain [unnamed] women." The only woman listed by name was Mary, the mother of Jesus. There is no doubt that women were frequently present among the followers of Jesus, but rarely were they named.

In spite of the fact that the world of the New Testament was a man's world and that even the Bible sometimes appears to accept the higher status of men, there can be no question about the crucial role women took in the early Christian church. In fact, women were included among the followers of Jesus from the beginning. The Gospels all indicate that women were often present with Jesus' companions.

James L. Mays makes an interesting observation when he says, "In contrast to the twelve male disciples, it is the women of the Bible who typically make the right response to Jesus" (Mays, 1978). Mays notes that the women who appear in the Gospel narratives most consistently model the life of service that is expected of followers of Jesus. He points to Peter's mother-in-law (Mark 1:29–31), who expressed her gratitude for Jesus' healing by serving. And there were the women who faithfully attended to the dead body of Jesus when all the male disciples were cowering in fear. That same pattern of service continued after the resurrection of Jesus and was evident in the early Christian church.

Women in Acts

In Acts there are a number of places where women as a group are mentioned. For example, Acts 8:1–3 describes Saul's persecution of the Christian church: "Saul was ravaging the church by entering house after house; dragging off both men and women, he committed them to prison" (v. 3). And Acts 9:2 says that Saul asked the high priest to provide letters to the synagogues so that if Saul "found any who belonged to the Way, men or women, he might bring them bound to Jerusalem." Apparently Saul was convinced that the women believers were just as great a threat as were the men. Women were just as dangerous as men when it came to telling the story of Jesus!

There are five stories in Acts in which individual women figure prominently (Acts 5:1–11; 9:36–43; 12:12–17; 16:11–15; 18:1–4, 18–28). We will look at the last two of these.

Lydia and the Women of Philippi (Acts 16:11–15)

This story takes place as Paul visits Philippi on his second missionary journey. But before we go on, a reminder about Paul is necessary. Paul was certainly a man of his time. He was born a Jew and grew up adhering to the beliefs of Judaism. He was a Roman citizen and so was also steeped in the traditions of Rome. Surely Paul was affected by the male-dominated society in which he was raised. Therefore, we should not be surprised when we see the conventional views about women reflected in Paul's writings (see 1 Cor. 11:2–16 and 14:33–36). The real surprises come in those times when Paul treated women or spoke about women in an unconventional way.

Most of the time when Paul arrived in a new city, he would go to the synagogue to meet with the worshiping community. That was where the men were; that was where he would meet the people of position and authority, the people who made the decisions. That's what Paul usually did, and that's what we would have expected when he arrived in Philippi.

 Want to Know More?

About the role of women during the time of the New Testament? See Evelyn and Frank Stagg, *Woman in the World of Jesus* (Philadelphia: Westminster Press, 1978); Carol A. Newsom and Sharon H. Ringe, eds. *Women's Bible Commentary,* Expanded Edition (Louisville: Ky.: Westminster John Knox Press, 1998), 482–88.

About purple? See Paul J. Achtemeier, ed., *Harper's Bible Dictionary* (San Francisco: Harper & Row, 1985), 844.

About house churches? See William H. Willimon, *Acts,* Interpretation, 39–42; Carolyn Osiek and David L. Balch, *Families in the New Testament World: Households and House Churches* (Louisville, Ky.: Westminster John Knox Press, 1997). For the modern movement of house churches, see J. G. Davies, ed., *The New Westminster Dictionary of Liturgy and Worship* (Philadelphia: Westminster Press, 1986), 260–62.

When Paul arrived in Philippi, however, the first thing he did comes as a shock. He went, not to the synagogue, but outside the city gates to the river, where there was a Sabbath gathering of women who had come together to pray.

An Aside: "Shall We Gather at the River . . ."

Luke provides us with an interesting detail when he mentions that they gathered at the *river* for prayer. I like the idea of gathering at the river for prayer. The river is a recurring symbol in the Bible. Psalm 1 says that the faithful person is like a tree planted by the rivers of water. Psalm 46 talks about a river that makes glad the city of God. Revelation 22:1 speaks of a river that flows out from the throne of God. And, of course, the Jordan River was where Jesus was baptized and where God said, "You are my beloved son" (Mark 1:9–11).

I was talking to friend who had been going through a rather stressful time, and needed some time away from it all to meditate and pray. So where did my friend go? To a place in the mountains with a sparkling stream flowing by. The experience was described like this: "Sitting there on the bank of the stream, it felt as if the water was carrying away my worries and fears and doubts. It was like the river was carrying my prayers to God."

"Gonna lay down my burdens, down by the riverside. . . ."

Perhaps that was the reason the people of Philippi chose the riverside as their place of prayer.

Lydia, a Worshiper of God and a Dealer in Purple Cloth

We don't know much about Lydia, but the few facts that Luke provides for us give an insight into the kind of person she was. First, she is identified as a worshiper of God. Apparently she was a Gentile who believed in God but was not a member of the Christian community. Her faith in God made her receptive to Paul's teaching, and she was so moved by the message she heard from Paul that she brought her whole family to be baptized. Lydia was Paul's first convert in Philippi.

Lydia is also identified as a seller of purple cloth, a luxury item that was sold exclusively to members of the upper class. (Luke's parable of the rich man and Lazarus begins with the rich man wearing purple; see Luke 16:19.) As a dealer in purple cloth, Lydia's business put her in contact with the elite of Philippi. In all likelihood, Lydia herself was wealthy. She was the head of her household.

As a demonstration of her conversion, Lydia opened her home to Paul. Her house apparently became the "house church" in Philippi (16:40), and the base of missionary activity in that city. Gail O'Day writes, "Lydia embodies Luke's ideal of women's contribution to the church: to provide housing and economic re-sources"(O'Day, 310).

One of the small miracles of this story of the conversion of Lydia is that she took the bold step of opening her home to Paul, and Paul took the equally bold step

> In the words of Kathleen Norris, only those "at home in themselves" can offer their home to others. See *Amazing Grace: A Vocabulary of Faith* (New York: Riverhead Books, 1998), 267.

of accepting her invitation. Here is an indication that the barriers that separated people out in the "real" world were being broken down in the church. In this one story we see the Christian community in Philippi made up of rich and poor, Gentile and Jew, male and female.

Priscilla and Aquila (18:1–4, 18–28)

We turn now to another story in which a woman plays a key part. Paul's missionary journey continued after his stay in Philippi, and it eventually brought him to Corinth, one of the great cities of Greece. Corinth was a major commercial center with seaports opening to both the Aegean Sea and the Adriatic Sea. As such a cosmopolitan city, it became a place where many immigrants settled. When Paul arrived in Corinth, he stayed in the home of a couple who had been expelled from Rome—Aquila and Priscilla. Interestingly, by the time Paul wrote his letter to the church at Rome several years later, Priscilla and Aquila had returned to Rome; we know this because Paul sends them his greet-ings at the end of the letter (Rom. 16:3).

The couple is always named together. Once Aquila is named first; twice Priscilla is named first. This could suggest that they were considered equals in their work in the church. More likely, Priscilla was the

> "Greet Prisca and Aquila, who work with me in Christ Jesus, and who risked their necks for my life, to whom not only I give thanks, but also all the churches of the Gen-tiles. Greet also the church in their house."
> —Romans 16:3–5a

stronger of the two. The normal convention would have been to name the man first, so Luke's decision to list Priscilla's name first could well have been because she was the better known to subsequent generations of Christians.

In addition to opening their home to Paul, Priscilla and Aquila became important coworkers with Paul. After some time in Corinth, Paul, Priscilla, and Aquila went to Ephesus. When Paul continued on, the couple stayed to oversee the missionary activities in that place.

> "If God cannot work through a religious institution, [God] will work around it."
> —Charles H. Talbert, *Acts,* Knox Preaching Guides, 80.

While in Ephesus, they heard an eloquent preacher named Apollos who was well versed in scripture, but whose message about Jesus was incomplete. Priscilla and Aquila "took him aside and explained the Way of God to him more accurately" (18:26). Any prohibition against women teachers that the church might have had obviously did not apply in every situation.

Priscilla served the church as a missionary and teacher, and her leadership in the young Christian church is undeniable.

The Church as a Model for the Kingdom Life

The Christian church of the first century blazed new ground. Rather than merely accepting the prevailing cultural ideas about socioeconomic barriers, racial barriers, and gender barriers, the church challenged and changed them. As the followers of Jesus attempted to live in response to Jesus' teachings, they discovered that the old way of looking at things simply didn't fit any more. Under the Lordship of Jesus, where there is "one faith, one baptism, one God and Father of us all" (Eph. 4:5), there is no room for divisions that set one person over another.

> "This faith is not simply about conversion nor is it only about wonder-working power; it is conversion into and power derived from a relationship with the risen Christ."—William H. Willimon, *Acts,* Interpretation, 148.

Even though we who are Christians are flawed and imperfect, we are, nevertheless, called to bear witness to the unity that is ours in Christ Jesus. The Christian church is an imperfect foreshadowing of the perfect life in the kingdom. That is still our mission today—to be a model for the kingdom life. We do that in many ways. Many of the same barriers that separated people in the first century continue to do so today. Socioeconomic, racial, and gender divisions set person against person and race against race. We, as followers of Jesus, are called to use our gifts to bring an end to the divisions that separate us one from another. One way we do this is in the language we choose. It is important to put into practice the use of language that hearkens to the kingdom where no such barriers exist.

We are the body of Christ in the world, and we have been called to point to a better way. Bold and courageous leaders are just as necessary now as twenty centuries ago.

? Questions for Reflection

1. In Acts 16:13, Paul speaks to a gathering of women by a river, at "a place of prayer." In that day and age, why would Paul choose to speak to the women? Why would a riverside be a place of prayer? Where are places of prayer for you?
2. The stories in these passages give examples of the early church breaking down barriers and blazing new ground. Where are the areas in today's society that offer the church the opportunity to break down barriers and blaze new ground?
3. From this unit and the previous one, we can ascertain that often Paul's style was to argue with people. Acts 18:4 mentions that he would go to the synagogue to argue on the sabbath, as if he attended in order to cause conflict. What would happen today if participants argued and debated during worship?
4. Priscilla and Aquila helped educate Apollos in the ways of the faith. Who are the individuals who educated or encouraged Christian faith in you?

Acts 19:1–41

A Riot in Ephesus

If there had been a tourist bureau in Ephesus in Paul's day, it would probably have included in its "must see" list of sites in Ephesus two things: the street magicians, and the temple of Artemis, the goddess of fertility. The travel brochure from the tourist bureau under "sites to see" would read:

> Street Magicians: No tour would be complete without stopping downtown and seeing some of the many street magicians plying their trade. Do you have a disease that needs curing or a curse to place on that certain enemy back home? The Magicians of Ephesus can take care of your every magic need. Our city is so well known for magic that in many parts of the world the word "Ephesian" is synonymous with magician.

And the brochure would have a beautiful picture of the Temple of Artemis with the following description:

> The Temple of Artemis: If your visit to Ephesus is brief, and you are able to see only one site, you will certainly not want to miss the Temple of Artemis, the goddess of fertility. People the world over come to see this beautiful temple and the statue of Artemis, which fell from heaven, on display inside the temple.

> Be sure to take advantage of the little shops around the temple where silver temple key chains, rings, and necklaces may be purchased from the fine Ephesian artisans. Small official shrines to Artemis may be purchased to be taken home, where you can set up your own Artemis worship center.

That was the Ephesus that Paul visited on his third missionary journey, and where he stayed for more than two years—a thriving seaport city and tourist attraction.

Paul Confronts the Magicians and the Silversmiths

It seems that every place Paul went he stirred things up. Some people thought of him as a troublemaker. At one point Paul and his fellow travelers were described as people who "are turning the world upside down" (Acts 17:6). What an appropriate description of Christians! That's what Christians do: they change things; they look at things in a new way; they turn things upside down.

Sometimes the changes the Christians brought were welcomed; other times they met with great resistance. There are some people who want their world turned upside down. People who have been victims of oppression are eager for someone to stand up against the oppression and turn that world of injustice upside down; the poor are eager for someone to help them meet their needs and turn their world of poverty upside down. But there are other people who regard this Christian influence as interference and a threat. These people are happy with things the way they are, and they don't want their world turned upside down.

> "These aristocratic magicians flee from Paul, humiliated, beaten, and stripped naked by the very spirit they tried to exorcise."—Paul W. Walaskay, *Acts*, Westminster Bible Companion, 180.

Paul encountered both groups during his time in Ephesus. Acts 19:11–20 tells about Paul's encounter with the famous magicians of Ephesus. Paul used the power of the Holy Spirit to outperform the magicians. When the magicians saw the mighty wonders that Paul did in the name of Jesus—healing people and driving out evil spirits—they knew at once that their trickery was nothing compared to the power of God. Paul's work was so impressive that many of the magicians gave up their magic. They gathered up their magic books (probably like recipe books for their various spells and incantations) and burned them publicly. Fifty thousand silver coins worth! The world of the magicians was turned upside down—turning away from superstition and magic to a belief in God. And "the word of the Lord grew mightily and prevailed" (Acts 19:20).

> "They are an example to us. They made the cleanest of clean cuts, even though it meant abandoning the things that were their livelihood. It is all too true that many of us hate our sins but either we cannot leave them at all or we do so with a lingering and backward look."—William Barclay, *Acts*, Daily Study Bible, 144.

When the silversmiths saw what Paul's work did to the magicians, they realized that his preaching could threaten their livelihood. These smiths did not want Paul turning their world upside down. Paul was preaching against gods made by human hands, saying that they were not real gods. His preaching scared the vendors around the temple who made their living selling silver idols, totems, and other trinkets for tourists to take home.

One of the anxious artisans, Demetrius, called a meeting of silversmiths and temple vendors. He said, "This Paul, who has already hurt the trade of the magicians, is now threatening us. If his preaching catches on, it's going to cost us some business. And, oh yeah, he may harm the worship of Artemis." Demetrius showed his true colors from the outset. He let us know from the beginning that this was all about money. And almost as an afterthought, he remembered to be indignant about the harm that might be done to the religion of Artemis.

He and the other artisans shrewdly realized that it would be more effective in stirring up the crowd to focus on Artemis, to make her the issue and not their income. They knew how important it was to put the right spin on it. (Today's "spin doctors" are practicing a skill that's been around a long time!) The artisans and vendors began to chant at the top of their lungs to get the people's attention, "Great is Artemis of the Ephesians." Before long a crowd was drawn to the shouting and commotion.

It is helpful to remember something about life in Ephesus two thousand years ago. There was no television, no movies, no video games, no telephones or radios, no cars to cruise around in, no air-conditioning to make it nice inside, nothing really going on. So it was certainly exciting and entertaining for there to be a disturbance about anything. Like a fight on the playground, something exciting was happening, and the whole population moved toward the action that was going on in the amphitheater of Ephesus. With all the confusion, a lot of people didn't even know why they were there; but no matter, it was obviously the place to be; it was where the action was. One speaker (Alexander) was put forward, but the crowd heckled him down. They started cheering, "Great is Artemis," which they continued to shout for two hours straight. If you look closely, you can almost see them doing the wave around the amphitheater.

"It was Super Bowl Sunday for Artemis."—Paul W. Walaskay, *Acts*, Westminster Bible Companion, 183.

Some people knew that Paul was the source of all of this, so they dragged some of Paul's companions out before the crowd. But where was Paul? The story says that he wanted to go out there in the middle of the crowd, but his followers would not let him. And it goes on to say that he even received some messages from others urging him not to go. The writer seems to be justifying Paul's absence to the reader who is surely asking, "Shouldn't Paul be out there, standing with his friends? Shouldn't he be standing up for his principles?" At the beginning of this passage we are told that Paul had resolved to go to Macedonia and Jerusalem and finally to Rome. Had he decided that his future plans were more important than standing for principle with his friends? Does this passage indicate that sometimes a person has to abandon one principle for another more important one? Is that justifiable?

Finally, when this riot starts getting out of hand, one of the city leaders, the town clerk, steps forward. He speaks a word of common sense, reminding those who can hear him in the crowd that if there is a real grievance it should be handled in the courts. And furthermore he warns them that if this disturbance continues, the Romans will come in and quiet it. The Romans, who ruled that part of the world, had a simple way of governing. As long as everything was quiet, they

> "He saved Paul and his companions but he saved them because he was saving his own skin."—William Barclay, *Acts,* Daily Study Bible, 147.

would leave people alone and allow them to live their lives and even practice their religion however they wanted. But at the first sign of trouble, the Romans would not mess around; they would put it down quickly and forcefully.

Word of what the clerk said gradually filtered up to the nosebleed section of the amphitheater. Everyone stopped being indignant; the chanting ceased, the wave died out, and everyone went home. End of story.

Contemporary Connections with the Story

The story of Paul's visit to Ephesus and the riot that ensued is a story that raises some intriguing issues that are pertinent two thousand years later. It illustrates how little things have changed over that time.

Isn't it amazing the role that money plays in our lives? Money is a driving motive for some people and they will go to great lengths to cover and protect their money, often disguising their motive. This is what the artisans did; they cloaked their fear of financial loss, portraying it as love for Artemis.

"Artemis, the multi-breasted, bountiful earth mother, was a goddess of banking and protector of debtors; and thus her worship was a syncretism of idolatrous religious devotion and economic interest . . . [and] has her devotees in every town, even today."—William H. Willimon, *Acts*, Interpretation, 152.

Crowd etiquette and crowd management seemed to have changed little also. Even today, the masses, out of boredom and the desire to be entertained, can be used for purposes they don't even understand.

And, as pointed out in this story, we each have to choose our battles. Like Paul, we have to decide whether a particular fight is the right one to die over. And the reasons or excuses for inaction continue today to sound like rationalizing (and perhaps they are rationalizing).

Notice also how the threat of personal cost can quell the enthusiasm of a crowd, a crowd that only seconds before appeared to be really caught up in the cause. How thin our resolve can be if there is even a hint of personal sacrifice. The little speech of the town clerk sends the crowd home.

Want to Know More?

About magic and magicians? See Donald K. McKim, *Westminster Dictionary of Theological Terms* (Louisville, Ky.: Westminster John Knox Press, 1996), 166, and Paul J. Achtemeier, ed., *Harper's Bible Dictionary* (San Francisco: Harper & Row, 1985), 594–96.

About the worship of Artemis? See Karel van der Toorn, Bob Becking, and Pieter W. van der Horst, eds., *Dictionary of Deities and Demons in the Bible,* 2nd revised ed. (Grand Rapids: Wm. B. Eerdmans Publishing Co., 1999), 91–97.

About Roman governance over its empire? See John E. Stambaugh and David L. Balch, *The New Testament in Its Social Environment,* Library of Early Christianity (Philadelphia: Westminster Press, 1986), 13–36.

Another point that makes this story memorable is its position in the book of Acts. This story is told in Acts 19, and it stands in stark contrast to what has gone before. For the preceding eighteen chapters the writer of Acts has been painting a picture of the early Christian church, a picture of the growth of the followers of Jesus, called "People of the Way." We've been reading about people who followed along Christ's way, and how their following led them to think about things in a whole new way. Someone once said that heaven is just a new pair of glasses (Lamott, 200). Kingdom glasses certainly led the early Christians to see things in a new way. They began to see their possessions in a whole new way; many sold their possessions and gave the money to the church so that no one would be in any need (Acts 4:32–37).

For eighteen chapters we've been reading about people who were willing to make great personal sacrifices for the sake of the gospel. We've been told about Stephen, who was put to death because of his faith in Jesus; we've heard about Barnabas and James and Philip and Peter and others whose faith in Jesus completely changed their way of looking at the world. For them the things that the world held valuable they now saw as being of little or no value. They had a whole new way of looking at things.

For eighteen chapters we've been reading about people whose faith in Jesus has brought about persecution and suffering and hardship. The writer has been painting a picture of the great lengths that the followers of Jesus have been willing to go on behalf of their Savior.

Against that backdrop of eighteen chapters of Christian generosity and giving and concern for the poor and devoted service, even at the cost of great personal sacrifice, now we come to chapter 19 and this picture of the people of Ephesus. It's a picture of selfishness, personal gain, and self-preservation. We can imagine those early Christian readers of the book of Acts shaking their heads at the silliness and pettiness of it all: Those Ephesians actually think that money is the most important thing. How sad! And they think that self preservation is important. How misguided! This picture that is painted of the Ephesians shows people who are so preoccupied with protecting their own self-interest and so concerned about saving themselves that they cannot see the true salvation that is theirs in Jesus Christ.

What this passage does for us is to set in contrast two pictures—one is a picture of the early Christian church that shows generosity, giving, sacrifice—and joy, peace, contentment, and happiness unlike anything they had ever experienced before. The other is a picture of the Ephesians that shows protection of self-interest, preoccupation with money, self-preservation—as well as fear, anxiety, loneliness, and an insecurity that had them constantly looking over their shoulders for where the next threat might come from.

> "Luke encourages the reader of this story to question the alliance between economics and religion, and to seek God who transcends all religion."—Paul W. Walaskay, *Acts*, Westminster Bible Companion, 184.

Maybe the reason this story has survived all these years is that in every generation those are the choices we face. Maybe the reason we continue to tell about the silliness of the people of Ephesus is that we too are prone to that same kind of silliness. Maybe what this story does for us is to turn our world upside down. Or is that right side up?

? Questions for Reflection

1. This unit places in tension two different worldviews: one that values generosity and personal sacrifice, and one that values self-interest and the accumulation of wealth. Are these the only two approaches to life? If not, what are some others? How would you characterize yourself? Why?

2. As with some of the previous passages in Acts, this passage makes a distinction about kinds of baptism—of John or Jesus, water or Spirit (Acts 19:1–6). What do you think is the difference between the two? Are both important? Why or why not?

3. The magicians burn their books in verse 19. Unfortunately for many of us, the image of book burning brings unpleasant reminders from history. Here though, it is probably intended as a positive statement. Why do you think they burned the books? What was the value of the books? What might be an accurate comparison of monetary value by today's standards? What are some examples today of ways that individuals make sacrifices for their faith?

4. "No little disturbance" broke out in Ephesus (v. 23). That's quite an understatement. What was the disturbance about? What are some parallels today of similar issues? How are these issues resolved? Perhaps Luke has crafted the story of the Ephesian crowd/riot as a smaller picture of the "no little disturbance" taking place throughout the whole narrative. How does one's witness to the gospel "disturb" the world?

10

Paul's Trial Before Agrippa

If you get a sense of *déjà vu* as you read these verses, it may be because it seems as if we have been here before. Chapters 25 and 26 tell about the trial of Paul before Governor Festus and King Agrippa, but it almost sounds like a repeat of the trial of Jesus before Governor Pilate and King Herod. Just like Jesus, Paul is bounced around between the various people in power. And, just as it was with Jesus, the people in power are the ones who in the end come off looking powerless and sad.

At his conversion (Acts 9:15), Paul was commissioned to carry the gospel to Gentiles and kings and the people of Israel. In this story today, he stands before the king. One of the regional governors, Festus, had just taken power, and he inherited Paul's case from his predecessor. Festus wasn't sure what to do about Paul. He read over Paul's case and couldn't find any offense worth referring to the emperor. By lucky coincidence, it happened that King Agrippa was coming to town. So Festus asked the King's advice. Paul was brought before Agrippa to tell his story.

King Agrippa and His Lovely Sister Bernice

King Agrippa's full name was Herod Agrippa II—yet another member of the powerful and ruthless Herod family. From the opening pages of the New Testament we have been dealing with various members of this family. King Agrippa was the great-grandson of Herod the Great, the one who ordered the slaughter of the innocent children when he learned about the birth of Jesus (see Matthew 2). Agrippa was the grandnephew of Herod Antipas, who beheaded John the

Baptist (Mark 6:17–29) and later was involved in the trial of Jesus (Luke 23:6–12). Agrippa was the son of Herod Agrippa I, who put to death James the disciple and persecuted the early church (Acts 12). Clearly, Agrippa came from a particularly hard-hearted family tree.

When Agrippa arrived in Caesarea, his sister Bernice accompanied him. Bernice herself was no model of virtue. After the death of her husband (who also happened to be her uncle!), she began an incestuous relationship with her brother Agrippa. That relationship continued in spite of another brief marriage and another affair. Obviously, Bernice believed that her position of power placed her above the standards of morality.

Paul was called to defend himself before Agrippa and Bernice. As Luke recounted the events, he made a point of the pomp and ceremony that surrounded the royal visit. As the processional entered, various courtiers and citizens bowed and scraped before the majesties. Only one person stood boldly before them—Paul.

Admittedly King Agrippa was a hard case. Some people might have concluded that Agrippa was simply a lost cause—why waste your breath on one such as he? But Paul was not like that. Paul never saw anyone as a lost cause. Perhaps it was because of his own experience. If he had been turned around, then he believed that anyone could be. So now that he was standing before the king—even a king like Agrippa—Paul was not going to miss an opportunity to tell about what Jesus had done in his life.

Paul's Defense (26:2–23)

Paul stood up, stretched out his hand (striking the pose of an orator), and began his speech. We might expect that Paul would give a reasoned theological statement, but instead, he tells a story. One of the characteristics of the Christian faith is that it demands to be expressed in a story. When we tell about what we believe, we do not use abstract concepts, we tell stories.

"Paul is about to present himself as victim of an internal Jewish squabble about the resurrection from the dead, an issue of "customs and controversies" that is hardly deserving of the sentence of death."—William H. Willimon, *Acts*, Interpretation, 176.

Standing before the king, Paul told his story about what Jesus had done in his life. The facts of Paul's story are well known, and need not be recited again. (We've read them twice already in Acts—chapter 9 and chapter 22.) One of the effects on us as we hear Paul recount these events once again is that we are given per-mission—and even encouraged—to tell our stories of how we have experienced Jesus' presence in our lives.

Personal testimonials have long been an important part of com-municating the faith. John Wesley told about the time on Aldersgate Street when he felt his heart "strangely warmed"; John Newton told about his experience of God's "amazing grace"; C. S. Lewis told about the night he stopped resisting God's steady advance and acknowl-edged God's presence in his life. (See *Conversions,* edited by Hugh Kerr and John Mulder, a collection of first-person accounts of the conversion experiences of a number of well-known religious figures through the history of the church. It is an inspiring and interesting book.) The Christian faith is passed from person to person through stories of personal experiences of God's grace.

As we read Paul's account, there is an authenticity and genuineness about it. It is in clear contrast to some of the stereotypical accounts of how "Jesus came into my life." Many of the stories told in revival meetings and on religious talk shows on TV follow a predictable formula: "I was miserable . . . I found Jesus . . . now my life is wonderful." Paul's speech before Agrippa, however, is considerably differ-ent from that tired recital. Nowhere does Paul describe his life before Jesus as

> "Luke goes to great lengths to demonstrate that nobody 'finds' Jesus. *Jesus finds us."*
> —William H. Willimon, *Acts,* Interpreta-tion, 180.

miserable, empty, or unfulfilled. By contrast, Paul was proud of his life (cf. Phil. 3:4–6). Also Paul makes it abundantly clear that he did not find Jesus; Jesus found him! As William Willimon says, "Most of the traffic on the bridge between us and God is moving toward us" (p. 180). And Paul's "wonderful life" after his encounter with Jesus was wonderful enough to include beatings, persecution, and impris-onment. Perhaps Paul's life was more like our lives. If so, Paul's speech gives Christians a valuable model for telling our faith stories.

Sharing the Faith: An Exercise

Even though the sharing of faith stories has been an important way of spreading the good news of the Gospel, there are many Christians today who have a difficult time putting their faith journey into words. To help you reflect on God's activity in your life, take a piece of paper and divide it into thirds. Let the paper become a time line of your life.

Think about your life in thirds. For example, if you are 45 years old, the first third of the page would be ages 1–15; the middle would be 16–30; the last third would be 31–45. Consider each of those time periods in your life. What would you list as the significant life events in each period, and how did you (or did you not) experience God's presence during each period?

Stop Kicking

Let's turn back to Paul and his defense before the king. Although the story of Paul's conversion has been told before in Acts, this particular account includes some words from Jesus not mentioned before. Having been blinded by the great light, Paul heard the voice from heaven saying, "Saul, Saul, why are you persecuting me? It hurts you to kick against the goads." The latter was a familiar Greek saying. A goad was a stick with a sharp point used to prod an uncooperative ox. Paul was that ox being prodded by God, and Paul was hurting himself when he attempted to go against God's will. Once again the Bible asserts that God's will is going to be done in the lives of people. As the Bible story is told, we see it time and again—Moses, Elijah, Jeremiah, Jonah all tried to resist God's will, only to be brought in line with God's plan for their lives. The truth is that God's will is going to be done!

> "His witness has not differed from that of the prophets and Moses. He is innocent because he has dared to proclaim only what faithful Israel has always proclaimed."—William H. Willimon, *Acts*, Interpretation, 178.

Almost Persuaded

Paul was making his defense when Festus interrupted. He'd heard enough. But Paul was not finished. He turned to the king and said, "King Agrippa, do you believe the prophets? I know that you believe." And the king responded, "Are you so quickly persuading me to become a Christian?" (26:28). The rendering of this verse in the King James Version says, "Almost thou persuadest me to be a Christian."

I think this is one of the saddest lines in the Bible. It's a sad contrast to what has gone before. Throughout the book of Acts we have been reading of people who have heard the good news of God's love and allowed that love to turn their lives around. We read about Peter's sermon at Pentecost when 3,000 people added their names to the followers of Jesus. We have read of the Philippian jailer who was about to commit suicide until Paul and Silas called out to him that all was well, and before the night was through, the jailer and his whole family were baptized. We have read about Lydia, the successful businesswoman, who became a Christian and a leader of the church. For twenty-six chapters we have read about people who heard the good news and allowed it to turn their lives in a whole new direction. We have grown accustomed to hearing of the successful spread of the gospel.

"Agrippa, listening to Paul, is more on trial than Paul is."—William Barclay, *Acts, Daily Study Bible,* 180.

But this time it is not so. When Agrippa finally speaks, he says, in effect, "You make a good argument . . . almost good enough to persuade me. But not quite." And with that Agrippa ships Paul off to Rome to be tried before the emperor.

Almost persuaded, but not quite. There is an old gospel hymn by that name, "Almost Persuaded."

> "Almost persuaded," now to believe;
> "Almost persuaded," Christ to receive;
> Seems now some soul to say, "Go, Spirit, go Thy way,
> Some more convenient day on Thee I'll call."

There is something about it that is heartbreaking. Almost . . . but not quite. And the person turns away. It brings to mind the rich man who came to Jesus and asked what he had to do to receive salvation, and when he was told what was expected of him, he went away sorrowful (Matt. 19:22). He just couldn't do it. Almost . . . but not quite.

I read about a conversation that took place between the late Clarence Jordan and his brother Robert. Clarence Jordan, the author of the Cotton Patch Version of the Gospels, was the founder of an interracial Christian cooperative in south Georgia known as Koinonia Farm. His brother Robert was an attorney who became a Georgia state senator and a justice of the Georgia Supreme Court. The exchange between these two brothers took place in the early '50s when Clarence came to ask his brother to provide some legal assistance for the controversial farm. Robert declined:

> "Clarence, I can't do that. You know my political aspirations. Why, if I represented you, I might lose my job, my house, everything I've got."
> "*We* might lose everything too, Bob."
> "It's different for you."

"Why is it different? I remember, it seems to me, that you and I joined the church the same Sunday, as boys. I expect when we came forward the preacher asked me about the same question he did you. He asked me, 'Do you accept Jesus as your Lord and Savior?' And I said, 'Yes.' What did you say?"

"I follow Jesus, Clarence, up to a point."

"Could that point by any chance be—the cross?"

"That's right. I follow him to the cross, but not *on* the cross. I'm not getting myself crucified."

"Then I don't believe you're a disciple. You're an admirer of Jesus, but not a disciple of his." (Cited in Dunham, 22)

Almost . . . but not quite.

I think that describes so many people, even many of us. We will follow to a point, but only to a point. The problem with being a disciple of Jesus is that it sometimes pushes us into some surprising places and into some situations that we would prefer to avoid. It sometimes forces us to rethink our values and to take our lives in a new direction. Being a disciple often puts us at a crossroads. Those crossroads moments come in big, momentous events of life, but most often they come in little, everyday situations. They come when we are making decisions about what to do with our time, what to do with our money; they come as we are making family decisions, business decisions.

> **Was Agrippa's question serious or just a joke?**
>
> "If sarcasm was intended, Paul ignored it with his response. He hopes that 'all who are listening'—and this includes all who read Luke's trial transcript—'might become such as I am'—a believer."—Paul W. Walaskay, *Acts*, Westminster Bible Companion, 230.

For example, you read in the church bulletin that volunteers are needed to help at the winter shelter. You wonder if you should sign up. But then you begin to have misgivings: you probably won't get a good night's sleep, and then you'll probably be irritable at work the next day. Besides somebody else will probably do it. So you let the opportunity pass. Almost . . . but not quite.

So many times we are in the same position as King Agrippa. So many times we have a chance to be disciples, to express our faith through our actions. We have a chance to reach out to someone in need, to be agents of God's love. We think about it . . . but, no, maybe later.

Here was King Agrippa so close to experiencing a whole new life. Almost . . . but not quite. And he turned away.

Epilogue for Agrippa?

This is the last we hear of King Agrippa. Almost persuaded . . . but not quite. It's one of the saddest stories in the Bible. Is that where it ends? Frederick Buechner has written:

> King Agrippa kept on being King Agrippa just as he always had. And yet you can't help wondering if somewhere inside himself the "almost" continued to live on as at least a sidelong glance down a new road, the faintest itching of the feet for a new direction. We don't know what happened to him after his brief appearance in the pages of Scripture. We certainly don't know what happened inside him. We can only pray for him—and also for ourselves—that in the absence of a sudden shattering event that turned some people around, there was a slow underground process that got him to the same place in the end. (Buechner, 31–32)

Want to Know More?

About some of the requirements of the Jewish legal system? See John E. Stambaugh and David L. Balch, *The New Testament in Its Social Environment*, Library of Early Christianity (Philadelphia: Westminster Press, 1986), 48–53, 97–102.

About persecution in the early church? See Ralph P. Martin and Peter H. Davids, eds., *Dictionary of the Later New Testament and Its Development* (Downers Grove, Ill.: InterVarsity Press, 1997), 907–14.

This is one of the truths of the gospel. Even though we may almost make the commitment, then turn away because it seems to require too much; even though we may turn from Jesus, he never turns away from us. And he never stops calling.

Unhindered? (Acts 28:30–31)

We cannot leave this study of Acts without looking at the closing verses. The first thing to say is that it's not much of an ending. Endings are supposed to pull together all the loose ends of the story and wrap everything up in a nice neat bow. But Luke doesn't do that. You almost expect that you could turn the page and continue reading. That is precisely Luke's intention. This story of the work of the Holy Spirit in the church did not end with the last verses of Acts; it is still being written even today. For twenty centuries faithful followers of Jesus have continued to add chapters to this ongoing story.

There is a wonderful truth in Luke's last word—"unhindered." When we left Paul, he was under house arrest, perhaps at times in chains. These sound like genuine hindrances. How can he be described as "unhindered"? Paul is unhindered because he is not the primary actor in this story; the Holy Spirit is. Caesar's chains may hinder Paul, but the Holy Spirit is unhindered. The Holy Spirit continues to work.

Luke was writing to a struggling band of Christians who faced persecution and hardship and sometimes surely felt that they were fighting a battle they could not win. The promise of Acts is that even in what seem to be the most "hindered" of circumstances, the Holy Spirit continues to work, and the good news continues to spread, and the church continues to grow. Even now we join the clouds of witnesses who have gone before us. Let us also join them in "proclaiming the kingdom of God and teaching about the Lord Jesus Christ with all boldness and without hindrance."

? Questions for Reflection

1. Contained within this unit is the suggestion for an exercise for a personal time line. Take a piece of paper and divide it into thirds. Let the paper represent a time line of your life. Divide your life into three equal sections. For example, if you are 45 years old, the first third of the page would be ages 1–15; the middle would be 16–30; the last third would be 31–45. Consider each of these time periods in your life. What would you list as the significant life events in each period, and how did you experience God's presence during each period?

2. Much is made in this unit about being persuaded to believe the gospel. What does it take to convince or persuade people to change their beliefs? Can one actually persuade someone else to believe in God, or is belief itself a part of God's grace? Why do you think so?

3. Compare the trial of Paul in this passage with the trial of Jesus in Luke 22:66–23:25. What are the similarities and differences?

4. The last words of the book of Acts are that Paul proclaimed and taught with "boldness and without hindrance" (28:31). Using a concordance, look up the words "bold," "boldly," and "boldness." Notice how often these words appear in Acts (and rarely elsewhere except in the letters of Paul). Look up these references. Who are the individuals that are described as "bold"? What happened to make them so bold?

Bibliography

Allinson, Francis Greenleaf. *Lucian, Satirist and Artist.* New York: Cooper Square Publishers, 1963.

Barclay, William. *The Acts of the Apostles.* Daily Study Bible. Philadelphia: Westminster Press, 1955.

————, *The Master's Men.* New York: Abingdon Press, 1959.

Bellah, Robert, et al. *Habits of the Heart: Individualism and Commitment in American Life.* New York: Harper & Row, 1985.

Bonhoeffer, Dietrich. *Life Together.* New York: Harper & Row, 1954.

Brown, Robert McAfee. *The Spirit of Protestantism.* New York: Oxford University Press, 1961.

Buechner, Frederick. *Whistling in the Dark: An ABC Theologized.* San Francisco: Harper & Row, 1988.

Carter, Jimmy. *Living Faith.* New York: Times Books, 1996.

Dunham, Robert E. "What Are You Taking on for Lent?" *Journal for Preachers,* Lent 1985.

Harvey, Andrew. *The Essential Mystics: The Soul's Journey into Truth.* London: HarperCollins, 1996.

Kerr, Hugh T., and John M. Mulder, eds. *Conversions.* Grand Rapids: Wm. B. Eerdmans Publishing Co., 1983.

Lamott, Anne. *Traveling Mercies.* New York: Pantheon Books, 1999.

Long, Thomas G. "A Night at the Burlesque: Wanderings through the Pentecost Narrative." *Journal for Preachers,* Pentecost 1991.

Mays, James Luther. ". . . And She Served Them." Union Theological Seminary in Virginia. *As I See It Today,* vol. 9, no. 2 (November 1978).

O'Day, Gail R. "Acts." In *Women's Bible Commentary,* Expanded Edition with Apocrypha. Edited by Carol A. Newsom and Sharon H. Ringe. Louisville: Westminster John Knox Press, 1998.

Niebuhr, H. Richard. "The Creation of Belief." *Cross Currents,* summer 1990.

Presbyterian Church (U.S.A.). *Book of Order 1998–99.* Louisville, Ky.: Office of the General Assembly, 1998.

Reid, T. R. *Confucius Lives Next Door: What Living in the East Teaches Us about Living in the West.* New York: Random House, 1999.

Shaffer, Peter. *Equus.* New York: Penguin Books, 1977.

Ten Boom, Corrie. *Tramp for the Lord.* Fort Washington, Pa.: Christian Literature Crusade, 1974.

Walaskay, Paul. *Acts.* Westminster Bible Companion. Louisville, Ky.: Westminster John Knox Press, 1998.

Willimon, William H. *Acts.* Interpretation. Atlanta: John Knox Press. 1988.

Interpretation Bible Studies
Leader's Guide

Interpretation Bible Studies (IBS), for adults and older youth, are flexible, attractive, easy-to-use, and filled with solid information about the Bible. IBS helps Christians discover the guidance and power of the scriptures for living today. Perhaps you are leading a church school class, a mid-week Bible study group, or a youth group meeting, or simply using this in your own personal study. Whatever the setting may be, we hope you find this *Leader's Guide* helpful. Since every context and group is different, this *Leader's Guide* does not presume to tell you how to structure Bible study for your situation. Instead, the *Leader's Guide* seeks to offer choices—a number of helpful suggestions for leading a successful Bible study using IBS.

> "The church that no longer hears the essential message of the Scriptures soon ceases to understand what it is for and is open to be captured by the dominant religious philosophy of the moment." —James D. Smart, *The Strange Silence of the Bible in the Church: A Study in Hermeneutics* (Philadelphia: Westminster Press, 1970), 10.

How Should I Teach IBS?

1. Explore the Format

There is a wealth of information in IBS, perhaps more than you can use in one session. In this case, more is better. IBS has been designed to give you a well-stocked buffet of content and teachable insights. Pick and choose what suits your group's needs. Perhaps you will want to split units into two or more sessions, or combine units into a single session. Perhaps you will decide to use only a portion of a unit and then move on to the next unit. *There is not a structured theme or teaching focus to each unit that must be followed for IBS to be used.* Rather, IBS offers the flexibility to adjust to whatever suits your context.

> "The more we bring to the Bible, the more we get from the Bible." —William Barclay, *A Beginner's Guide to the New Testament* (Louisville, Ky.: Westminster John Knox Press, 1995), vii.

A recent survey of both professional and volunteer church educators revealed that their number one concern was that Bible study materials be teacher-friendly. IBS is, indeed teacher-friendly in two important ways. First, since IBS provides abundant content and a flexible design, teachers can shape the lessons creatively, responding to the needs of the group and employing a wide variety of teaching methods. Second, those who wish more specific suggestions for planning the sessions can find them at the Geneva Press web site on the Internet (**www.ppcpub.org**). Click the "IBS Teacher Helps" button to access teaching suggestions for each IBS unit as well as helpful quotations, selections from Bible dictionaries and encyclopedias, and other teaching helps.

IBS is not only teacher-friendly, it is also discussion-friendly. Given the opportunity, most adults and young people relish the chance to talk about the kind of issues raised in IBS. The secret, then, is to determine what works with your group, what will get them to talk. Several good methods for stimulating discussion are presented in this *Leader's Guide,* and once you learn your group, you can apply one of these methods and get the group discussing the Bible and its relevance in their lives.

The format of every IBS unit consists of several features:

a. Body of the Unit. This is the main content, consisting of interesting and informative commentary on the passage and scholarly insight into the biblical text and its significance for Christians today.

b. Sidebars. These are boxes that appear scattered throughout the body of the unit, with maps, photos, quotations, and intriguing ideas. Some sidebars can be identified quickly by a symbol, or icon, that helps the reader know what type of information can be found in that sidebar. There are icons for illustrations, key terms, pertinent quotes, and more.

c. Want to Know More? Each unit includes a "Want to Know More?" section that guides learners who wish to dig deeper and consult other resources. If your church library does not have the resources mentioned, you can look up the information in other standard Bible dictionaries, encyclopedias, and handbooks, or you can find much of this information at the Geneva Press Web site (see last page of this Guide).

d. Questions for Reflection. The unit ends with questions to help the learners think more deeply about the biblical passage and its pertinence for today. These questions are provided as examples only, and teachers are encouraged both to develop their own list of questions and to gather questions from the group. These discussion questions do not usually have specific "correct" answers. Again, the flexibility of IBS allows you to use these questions at the end of the group time, at the beginning, interspersed throughout, or not at all.

> "The trick is to make the Bible our book." — Duncan S. Ferguson, *Bible Basics: Mastering the Content of the Bible* (Louisville, Ky.: Westminster John Knox Press, 1995), 3.

2. Select a Teaching Method

Here are ten suggestions. The format of IBS allows you to choose what direction you will take as you plan to teach. Only you will know how your lesson should best be designed for your group. Some adult groups prefer the lecture method, while others prefer a high level of free-ranging discussion. Many youth groups like interaction, activity, the use of music, and the chance to talk about their own experiences and feelings. Here is a list of a few possible approaches. Let your own creativity add to the list!

a. Let's Talk about What We've Learned. In this approach, all group members are requested to read the scripture passage and the IBS unit before the group meets. Ask the group members to make notes about the main issues, concerns, and questions they see in the passage. When the group meets, these notes are collected, shared, and discussed. This method depends, of course, on the group's willingness to do some "homework."

b. What Do We Want and Need to Know? This approach begins by having the whole group read the scripture passage together. Then, drawing from your study of the IBS, you, as the teacher, write on a board or flip chart two lists:

(1) Things we should know to better understand this passage (content information related to the passage, for example, historical insights about political contexts, geographical landmarks, economic nuances, etc.), and

> "Although small groups can meet for many purposes and draw upon many different resources, the one resource which has shaped the life of the Church more than any other throughout its long history has been the Bible." —Roberta Hestenes, *Using the Bible in Groups* (Philadelphia: Westminster Press, 1983), 14.

(2) Four or five "important issues we should talk about regarding this passage" (with implications for today— how the issues in the biblical context continue into today, for example, issues of idolatry or fear).

Allow the group to add to either list, if they wish, and use the lists to lead into a time of learning, reflection, and discussion. This approach is suitable for those settings where there is little or no advanced preparation by the students.

c. Hunting and Gathering. Start the unit by having the group read the scripture passage together. Then divide the group into smaller clusters (perhaps having as few as one person), each with a different assignment. Some clusters can discuss one or more of the "Questions for Reflection." Others can look up key terms or people in a Bible dictionary or track down other biblical references found in the body of the unit. After the small clusters have had time to complete their tasks, gather the entire group again and lead them through the study material, allowing each cluster to contribute what it learned.

d. From Question Mark to Exclamation Point. This approach begins with contemporary questions and then moves to the biblical content as a response to those questions. One way to do this is for you to ask the group, at the beginning of the class, a rephrased version of one or more of the "Questions for Reflection" at the end of the study unit. For example, one of the questions at the end of the unit on Exodus 3:1–4:17 in the IBS *Exodus* volume reads,

> Moses raised four protests, or objections, to God's call. Contemporary people also raise objections to God's call. In what ways are these similar to Moses' protests? In what ways are they different?

This question assumes familiarity with the biblical passage about Moses, so the question would not work well before the group has explored the passage. However, try rephrasing this question as an opening exercise; for example:

Here is a thought experiment: Let's assume that God, who called people in the Bible to do daring and risky things, still calls people today to tasks of faith and courage. In the Bible, God called Moses from a burning bush and called Isaiah in a moment of ecstatic worship in the Temple. How do you think God's call is experienced by people today? Where do you see evidence of people saying "yes" to God's call? When people say "no" or raise an objection to God's call, what reasons do they give (to themselves, to God)?

Posing this or a similar question at the beginning will generate discussion and raise important issues, and then it can lead the group into an exploration of the biblical passage as a resource for thinking even more deeply about these questions.

e. Let's Go to the Library. From your church library, your pastor's library, or other sources, gather several good commentaries on the book of the Bible you are studying. Among the trustworthy commentaries are those in the Interpretation series (John Knox Press) and the Westminster Bible Companion series (Westminster John Knox Press). Divide your group into smaller clusters and give one commentary to each cluster (one or more of the clusters can be given the IBS volume instead of a full-length commentary). Ask each cluster to read the biblical passage you are studying and then to read the section of the commentary that covers that passage (if your group is large, you may want to make photocopies of the commentary material with proper permission, of course). The task of each cluster is to name the two or three most important insights they discover about the biblical passage by reading and talking together about the commentary material. When you reassemble the larger group to share these insights, your group will gain not only a variety of insights about the passage but also a sense that differing views of the same text are par for the course in biblical interpretation.

f. Working Creatively Together. Begin with a creative group task, tied to the main thrust of the study. For example, if the study is on the Ten Commandments, a parable, or a psalm, have the group rewrite the Ten Commandments, the parable, or the psalm in contemporary language. If the passage is an epistle, have the group write a letter to their own congregation. Or if the study is a narrative, have the group role-play the characters in the story or write a page describing the story from the point of view of one of the characters. After completion of the task, read and discuss the biblical passage, asking for interpretations and applications from the group and tying in IBS material as it fits the flow of the discussion.

g. Singing Our Faith. Begin the session by singing (or reading) together a hymn that alludes to the biblical passage being studied (or to the theological themes in the passage). Most hymnals have an index of scriptural allusions. For example, if you are studying the unit from the IBS volume on Psalm 121, you can sing "I to the Hills Will Lift My Eyes," "Sing Praise to God, Who Reigns Above," or another hymn based on Psalm 121. Let the group reflect on the thoughts and feelings evoked by the hymn, then move to the biblical passage, allowing the biblical text and the IBS material to underscore, clarify, refine, and deepen the discussion stimulated by the hymn. If you are ambitious, you may ask the group to write a new hymn at the end of the study! (Many hymnals have indexes in the back or companion volumes that help the user match hymns to scripture passages or topics.)

h. Fill in the Blanks. In order to help the learners focus on the content of the biblical passage, at the beginning of the session ask each member of the group to read the biblical passage and fill out a brief questionnaire about the details of the passage (provide a copy for each learner or write the questions on the board). For example, if you are studying the unit in the IBS *Matthew* volume on Matthew 22:1–14, the questionnaire could include questions such as the following:

—In this story, Jesus compares the kingdom of heaven to what?
—List the various responses of those who were invited to the king's banquet but who did not come.
—When his invitation was rejected, how did the king feel? What did the king do?
—In the second part of the story, when the king saw a man at the banquet without a wedding garment, what did the king say? What did the man say? What did the king do?
—What is the saying found at the end of this story?

Gather the group's responses to the questions and perhaps encourage discussion. Then lead the group through the IBS material helping the learners to understand the meanings of these details and the significance of the passage for today. Feeling creative? Instead of a fill-in-the blanks questionnaire, create a crossword puzzle from names and words in the biblical passage.

i. Get the Picture. In this approach, stimulate group discussion by incorporating a painting, photograph, or other visual object into the lesson. You can begin by having the group examine and comment on this visual or you can introduce the visual later in the lesson—it depends on the object used. If, for example, you are studying the unit Exodus 3:1–4:17 in the IBS *Exodus* volume, you may want to view Paul Koli's very colorful painting *The Burning Bush.* Two sources for this painting are *The Bible Through Asian Eyes,* edited by Masao Takenaka and Ron O'Grady (National City, Calif.: Pace Publishing Co., 1991), and *Imaging the Word: An Arts and Lectionary Resource,* vol. 3, edited by Susan A. Blain (Cleveland: United Church Press, 1996).

j. Now Hear This. Especially if your class is large, you may want to use the lecture method. As the teacher, you prepare a presentation on the biblical passage, using as many resources as you have available plus your own experience, but following the content of the IBS unit as a guide. You can make the lecture even more lively by asking the learners at various points along the way to refer to the visuals and quotes found in the "sidebars." A place can be made for questions (like the ones at the end of the unit)—either at the close of the lecture or at strategic points along the way.

> "It is . . . important to call a Bible study group back to what the text being discussed actually says, especially when an individual has gotten off on some tangent." —Richard Robert Osmer, *Teaching for Faith: A Guide for Teachers of Adult Classes* (Louisville, Ky.: Westminster John Knox Press, 1992), 71.

3. Keep These Teaching Tips in Mind

There are no surefire guarantees for a teaching success. However, the following suggestions can increase the chances for a successful study:

a. Always Know Where the Group Is Headed. Take ample time beforehand to prepare the material. Know the main points of the study, and know the destination. Be flexible, and encourage discussion, but don't lose sight of where you are headed.

b. Ask Good Questions; Don't Be Afraid of Silence. Ideally, a discussion blossoms spontaneously from the reading of the scripture. But more often than not, a discussion must be drawn from the group members by a series of well-chosen questions. After asking each question, give the group members time to answer. Let them think, and don't be threatened by a season of silence. Don't feel that every question must have an answer, and that as leader, you must supply every answer. Facilitate discussion by getting the group members to cooperate with each other. Sometimes, the original question can be restated. Sometimes it is helpful to ask a follow-up question like "What makes this a hard question to answer?"

Ask questions that encourage explanatory answers. Try to avoid questions that can be answered simply "Yes" or "No." Rather than asking, "Do you think Moses was frightened by the burning bush?" ask, "What do you think Moses was feeling and experiencing as he stood before the burning bush?" If group members answer with just one word, ask a follow-up question like "Why do you think this is so?" Ask questions about their feelings and opinions, mixed within questions about facts or details. Repeat their responses or restate their response to reinforce their contributions to the group.

"Studies of learning reveal that while people remember approximately 10% of what they hear, they remember up to 90% of what they say. Therefore, to increase the amount of learning that occurs, increase the amount of talking about the Bible which each member does."—Roberta Hestenes, *Using the Bible in Groups* (Philadelphia: Westminster Press, 1983), 17.

Most studies can generate discussion by asking open-ended questions. Depending on the group, several types of questions can work. Some groups will respond well to content questions that can be answered from reading the IBS comments or the biblical passage. Others will respond well to questions about feelings or thoughts. Still others will respond to questions that challenge them to new thoughts or that may not have exact answers. Be sensitive to the group's dynamic in choosing questions.

Some suggested questions are: What is the point of the passage? Who are the main characters? Where is the tension in the story? Why does it say (this)_____, and not (that) _____? What raises questions for you? What terms need defining? What are the new ideas? What doesn't make sense? What bothers or troubles you about this passage? What keeps you from living the truth of this passage?

c. Don't Settle for the Ordinary. There is nothing like a surprise. Think of special or unique ways to present the ideas of the study. Upset the applecart of the ordinary. Even though the passage may be familiar, look for ways to introduce suspense. Remember that a little mystery can capture the imagination. Change your routine.

Along with the element of surprise, humor can open up a discussion. Don't be afraid to laugh. A well-chosen joke or cartoon may present the central theme in a way that a lecture would have stymied.

Sometimes a passage is too familiar. No one speaks up because everyone feels that all that could be said has been said. Choose an unfamiliar translation from which to read, or if the passage is from a Gospel, compare the story across two or more Gospels and note differences. It is amazing what insights can be drawn from seeing something strange in what was thought to be familiar.

d. Feel Free to Supplement the IBS Resources with Other Material. Consult other commentaries or resources. Tie in current events with the lesson. Scour newspapers or magazines for stories that touch on the issues of the study. Sometimes the lyrics of a song, or a section of prose from a well-written novel will be just the right seasoning for the study.

e. And Don't Forget to Check the Web. Check out our site on the World Wide Web (www.ppcpub.org). Click the "IBS Teacher Helps" button to access teaching suggestions. Several possibilities for applying the teaching methods suggested above for individual IBS units will be available. Feel free to download this material.

> "The Bible is literature, but it is much more than literature. It is the holy book of Jews and Christians, who find there a manifestation of God's presence." —Kathleen Norris, *The Psalms* (New York: Riverhead Books, 1997), xxii.

f. Stay Close to the Biblical Text. Don't forget that the goal is to learn the Bible. Return to the text again and again. Avoid making the mistake of reading the passage only at the beginning of the study, and then wandering away to comments on top of comments from that point on. Trust in the power and presence of the Holy Spirit to use the truths of the passage to work within the lives of the study participants.

What If I Am Using IBS in Personal Bible Study?

If you are using IBS in your personal Bible study, you can experiment and explore a variety of ways. You may choose to read straight through the study without giving any attention to the sidebars or

other features. Or you may find yourself interested in a question or unfamiliar with a key term, and you can allow the sidebars "Want to Know More?" and "Questions for Reflection" to lead you into deeper learning on these issues. Perhaps you will want to have a few commentaries or a Bible dictionary available to pursue what interests you. As was suggested in one of the teaching methods above, you may want to begin with the questions at the end, and then read the Bible passage followed by the IBS material. Trust the IBS resources to provide good and helpful information, and then follow your interests!

Want to Know More?

About leading Bible study groups? See Roberta Hestenes, *Using the Bible in Groups* (Philadelphia: Westminster Press, 1983).

About basic Bible content? See Duncan S. Ferguson, *Bible Basics: Mastering the Content of the Bible* (Louisville, Ky.: Westminster John Knox Press, 1995); William M. Ramsay, *The Westminster Guide to the Books of the Bible* (Louisville, Ky.: Westminster John Knox Press, 1994).

About the development of the Bible? See John Barton, *How the Bible Came to Be* (Louisville, Ky.: Westminster John Knox Press, 1997).

About the meaning of difficult terms? See Donald K. McKim, *Westminster Dictionary of Theological Terms* (Louisville, Ky.: Westminster John Knox Press, 1996); Paul J. Achtemeier, *Harper's Bible Dictionary* (San Francisco: Harper & Row, 1985).

For more information about IBS,
click the "IBS Teacher Helps" button at
www.ppcpub.org